MW01709042

The Only Gospel That Saves

All Others Condemn To Hell

Milton Edwards

ISBN: 978-1-60383-551-0

Published by:

Holy Fire Publishing

www.HolyFirePublishing.com

Cover Design: Jay Cookingham

Printed in the United States of America, The United Kingdom and Australia

TABLE OF CONTENTS

PREFACE

My prayer for all who read this book is that they will understand the saving gospel of our Lord and Savior Jesus Christ and be saved. I see so many people going to church faithfully but are not saved. When asked about their reason for their hope in making it to heaven, they say: "I think I'm a good person" or "I believe in Jesus, I accepted Him into my heart."

These reasons show that they are not saved according to the gospel. Their lives also don't show the new nature of holiness and godliness, as being evidence of the Holy Spirit living in them. They are seeking earthly things and are not seeking "those things from above" as stated in **Colossians 3:1–2,** and have no desire to "know him, and the power of his resurrection, and the fellowship of his sufferings, being made conformable unto his death." **Philippians 3:10**

Jesus says in **John 3:3** "Except a man be born again, he cannot see the kingdom of God." This means trusting in your own goodness and law-keeping will not save you. You must be born again! This is not something that you do, but what God does for you when you truly repent and believe in Jesus.

I pray that the Lord save you, guide you, and preserve you blameless and spotless until His appearing when you will stand before the presence of His glory with exceeding joy and not in terror, in Jesus' name, Amen.

CHAPTER 1

THE ONLY GOSPEL THAT SAVES MESSAGE

With the famous verse of **John 3:16** constantly preached in reminding us of the love of God, we forget the entire gospel message. If you look at the passage closely, from which this was taken, you will see that judgment is also a part of the gospel message for rejecting Christ. But most churches shy away from declaring the full message. **John 3:18** tells us that he who believes in Jesus Christ has eternal life, but he who does not believe has eternal damnation.

Although God demonstrated His love toward us by sending His Son Jesus Christ to pay for our sins, we must repent and believe in Him to receive eternal life. If we don't, we will perish.

Even though Christ already finished the work of salvation on our behalf, this does not mean that we all automatically go to heaven when Jesus returns. The Bible tells us in the book of Revelation, "that whosoever is thirsty; let him take of the water of life freely." You must take of the water of life to have eternal life.

To believe in Jesus means that you must do what He has commanded you to do: take up your cross daily, deny yourself and follow Him. You cannot follow your desires of worldly lusts and pleasures and expect to go to heaven, just because you have been told that Jesus already died to pay for the sins of the world. You must make God's will and kingdom the number one priority in your life, not your will.

Entering the kingdom of God is not as easy as many preachers proclaim. Sin is a very huge barrier that will prevent many from entering. Although Jesus paid the price for the redemption of sinners, we also have a price to pay if we choose to follow Him. Most of us don't want to forsake all and follow Jesus to enter heaven, and that's the problem.

It is obvious from the passage of **John 3:18**, that the love God displayed in sending His Son to die on the cross for our sins, tells us that sin is very serious, and the consequence for rejecting the sacrifice Jesus made for it is everlasting torment in a lake of fire: a very serious eternal penalty.

Jesus died for a reason that has eternal significance. The eternity of man depends on the sacrifice of Christ, whether heaven or hell. He did not die in vain. He died because the Law could not save us; it condemned us to eternal death. As the Apostle Paul says in **Galatians 2:21**, "If righteousness came by the law, then Christ died in vain." But Jesus did not die in vain.

I pray that we will all think very carefully about the death, burial, and resurrection of Christ, and consider it with all our heart, mind, and soul. Don't just let the message of the cross go through one ear and out the other; think about the reasons Jesus died. Your eternity hangs on the cross of Christ, and that's the greatest reason to consider it highly above all things.

Don't forget the justice and righteousness of God also demonstrated in the cross. Don't let the love of God be the sum of the cross. Judgment was also demonstrated. As the Apostle Paul also states in **Romans 3:26**, "that God might be just and the justifier of him who believes in Jesus." Did you hear what Paul said in the book of Romans: that God might be just? This means that the cross demonstrated the justice of God against sins.

Did you also hear what Paul said in **Romans 1** that "Christ is the righteousness of God revealed from faith to faith?" This also means that only in the cross is the righteousness of God revealed. In other words, the cross truly reveals how terrible sin is and what it cost a thrice holy God to remove it from us to justify us as righteous. Therefore, the cross shows more than just the love of God; it shows also His justice.

Unfortunately, the very familiar "love of God" gospel message has overshadowed "the judgment of God" part of the message, and pastors are not preaching the entire gospel. What happens if a person chooses not to follow Christ? Can they choose another way to God and still avoid hell?

Many preachers today are not explaining fully the cross to the unsaved. Questions like the following must be fully explained so that people see their absolute need for Christ:

If God loved us so much, why did He have to send His only begotten Son to die? Why couldn't God just forgive our sins and give us eternal life? Does it make any sense that God loves us so much that He had to put His Son to death to display that love?

The Bible tells us that the seriousness of sin was the reason God had to send His only begotten Son to die on the cross to rescue us from eternal judgment, and that there was no other way forgiveness of sins could be granted. This truth of the cross shows how truly serious sin is in God's eyes, even though those who reject the cross think differently on sin. Despite what they think of sin, the cross already shows God's view, and that's what matters and will ultimately prevail on Judgment Day.

Today, there are so many different interpretations of the gospel, that it has become very difficult for those who don't know the truth; to believe that there is only one true absolute gospel message. This confusion was not brought about by God, but the Devil and his deceitful ministers, who desire to lead men to destruction through the preaching of a different gospel.

God gave a simple gospel so that all men will hear and understand. This does not mean they will accept it, but He has already made it plain so that all men will come to the saving knowledge of Jesus Christ. Why would God send His Son to die for the sins of mankind and then make it confusing? Who would ever trust a God like that? But God is not like that; God has demonstrated His mercy towards mankind by the way of the cross. The cross is more than sufficient to express God's mercy. What amazing love!

But His wrath against sins first had to be carried out before His love could be poured out through the gift of His Holy Spirit. What I mean is, there is a gospel that tells only about the love of God without first explaining sin and its penalty. This is the most widely preached gospel today, and it does not give the full counsel of God: His wrath and judgment against sin.

The only-love gospel is more of a seducing spirit; a spirit that is all about love without judgment. It's almost like the homosexual marriages that are done by certain churches based on love. Their logic is that if Tom loves Harry then that's all God cares about. No, that's a big lie and scripture-twisting of God's Word. God says that same-sex relationship is an abomination, not a commendation.

Now, we have fallen into the love trap also with the gospel as we have with marriages. I'm not against love. I'm just against certain kinds of ungodly so-called "love" that claims God's approval, not knowing that God's judgment is already set against their sinful works.

Well, I'm sorry to say this, but God is a God of judgment. This attribute of God is widely proclaimed in the Bible, from Old to New Testament. How could we leave this out? How could we make up another God of our own liking?

We can't just say to sinners, Jesus loves you, without showing them their present condition before God: sinners who stand condemned and guilty before God, ready to be cast into eternal hell. We must explain to them the absolute vital need to repent and be converted; we must tell them that they must become new creatures in Christ.

We are now in an age of many false teachers and corrupters of the gospel, that the good news of the cross doesn't even seem like good news anymore. It has become more like an old fable. The death of Christ has been taken for granted, when it's in fact very serious business. So serious is the gospel that it is eternal. The penalty for not obeying it is everlasting destruction with weeping and gnashing of teeth; no rest day or night. The reward for obeying it is everlasting life with God and unspeakable joy; no more tears and pain.

The Bible tells us that there is only one gospel. If any angel or person comes with any other interpretation, let him be accursed to everlasting destruction. For this reason, we should know what the gospel is: the full message.

The gospel message is so absolute that the warning of eternal destruction is pronounced against those who pervert it. This warning is repeated twice in **Galatians 1:8–9**, then in **Jude 1**, and **2 Peter 2**, as well as in other Scriptures.

Galatians 1:7–9: *Which is not another; but there be some that trouble you, and would pervert the gospel of Christ.*

But though we, or an angel from heaven, preach any other gospel unto you than that which we have preached unto you, let him be accursed. As we said before, so say I now again, if any man preach any other gospel unto you than that ye have received, let him be accursed.

He also warned us about another Jesus and another spirit.

Which Jesus do you believe in or which spirit have you received?

2 Corinthians 11:4: *For if he that cometh preacheth another Jesus, whom we have not preached, or if ye receive another spirit, which ye have not received, or another gospel, which ye have not accepted, ye might well bear with him.*

Why would the Apostle Paul repeat this warning so many times if perversion of the true message of the cross wasn't very serious? This message is so serious that if you get it wrong, you will end up in the lake of fire forever in torment. Don't you think that's very serious?

Jesus already warned that many would try to enter heaven, but they will not be able to, because the way is straight and narrow and few will find it. These other gospels are the ways in which Jesus meant many people would try to enter heaven but will find the door shut.

CHAPTER 2

THE CROSS OF CHRIST FULLY DEMONSTRATES GOD'S HOLY NATURE

Does the Bible say that God is only love? Is that the full nature of God?

We have always heard the verse of **St. John 3:16** quoted frequently as the gospel message, declaring that God is love. We have been told that God's nature is love and that's why He sent His only begotten Son into the world to save us from sins. But let us not forget that God's nature is that He is holy. Comprising that nature is the attribute of love.

God is holy, that's why He hates sin. He could not allow sin and death to reign any longer, so He put an end to it when He sent His Son Jesus to conquer it and bring about everlasting righteousness, giving us eternal life.

However, sin allows God to display His full nature of mercy, love, longsuffering, kindness, wrath, judgment, etc. If there were no sin, we would not understand the amazing love and mercy of God. While the cross demonstrates the love of God, it also fully demonstrates His holiness and righteousness.

Now, if God were only love, without demonstrating His judgment against sins according to His holiness, why did Jesus have to suffer such a terrible death on the cross to demonstrate God's amazing love? If love was the total sum of the full nature of God, why couldn't we be forgiven of sins without Christ being put to death?

Although God is love, let us not forget what that love is. God's love is not like our love. His love is holy love. This means that judgment for sin must be fully paid, satisfactory and well- pleasing in His sight. As His Word declares, the wages of sin is death (Romans 6:23). So, in view of God's holiness, His Law declares that our just and fair judgment for sin is death.

Sin is God's enemy. It wants to take the position of God. It desires to reign as king. It's rebellion against God, the True and Eternal King, Who alone is worthy to reign and rule in righteousness. We are told in the book of Romans that when Christ died and rose from the dead, He did it so that sin and death would no longer reign, but righteousness and eternal life.

Jesus came to defeat sin so that it would no longer exalt itself above the righteousness and holiness of God. So, that God, who is the Eternal King, the Alpha and Omega, with neither beginning nor ending, would forever reign in righteousness.

Romans 5:21: *That as sin hath reigned unto death, even so might grace reign through righteousness unto eternal life by Jesus Christ our Lord.*

Why did God choose to grant us mercy by not giving us the wrath we deserved, but provided the spotless eternal substitute (Jesus Christ), who would take our punishment for sins?

The Bible says that God loved the world so much that He gave His only begotten Son to die. Jesus says that His Father loves Him because He laid down His life for His friends. The love of God for us is fully demonstrated in the sufferings of Christ for our sins.

Apart from the death, burial, and resurrection of Christ, God's nature could not be kept pure and holy. If God had forgiven us of our sins without having a just sacrifice to satisfy His justice against sins, His holiness would be corrupted, making Him less holy than He is. For this cause, the Bible says that God loved the world so much that He gave up His only begotten Son to suffer on the cross to pay for our sins to give us eternal life.

It is because of God's love and compassion towards us, not willing that we would eternally perish, that led Him to give Jesus Christ, the Holy One, to suffer humiliation, insults, and other injustices at the hands of sinners, and then finally, crucifixion for us. But wrapped up in this love was also His justice and judgment against sins.

Knowing that God is holy and against sin is what makes His love towards sinners so amazing. It is a wonder that God, who is so holy, would pay such a price to adopt sinners into His heavenly kingdom; that is the nature of God's love!

The fact is we were already condemned to everlasting fire like the devil and His angels, but God, in His great love and mercy for us, gave up His Son to be the just payment for our sins. Therefore, God's love cost Him the life of His Only Son—His greatest treasure!

John 3:16: *For God so loved the world, that he gave his only begotten Son, that whosoever believeth in him should not perish, but have everlasting life.*

John 10:17: *Therefore doth my Father love me, because I lay down my life, that I might take it again.*

John 15:13: *Greater love hath no man than this, that a man lay down his life for his friends.*

The sacrifice of Christ demonstrates a love that is far beyond our imagination. The Bible tells us that all of us are enemies of God and children of the wrath of God by default—our sinful nature inherited through the fall of Adam. But God made a way for us to have eternal life and to avoid His wrath, and that way was through the cross of Christ.

How amazing is it for someone to die for his friends, just to demonstrate his amazing love? That's what makes the cross so amazing! And that's how God demonstrated His amazing love, righteousness, holiness, longsuffering, forgiveness, patience, kindness, goodness, etc., towards us.

Now, this love is shed abroad by the Holy Spirit, given only to those who have accepted Jesus Christ as Son of God, Lord, Savior, and have given up everything to follow Him.

Jesus says that His Father loves Him because He laid down His life for

His friends, and that there is no greater love than that. Now, what do you think of this kind of love, a love that cost the life of the Son of God? Does this love sound like our kind of love? Since God demonstrated His love towards us through the death of His Son, we are also commanded to demonstrate our love for the brethren by also laying our lives down.

1 John 3:16: *Hereby perceive we the love of God, because he laid down his life for us: and we ought to lay down our lives for the brethren.*

But why is the laying down of one's life the demonstration of God's love? Why was the death of Christ necessary to display the love of God? It is because of the holiness of God. God's nature is that He is holy. In relation to sin, love is not the full nature of God; holiness is.

Love is only a part of the full picture. God loves us, His chosen people, but He hates our sins. The Bible repeatedly tells us that God loves the righteous but hates the wicked. God will reward the righteous in heaven while punishing the wicked in hell.

For those who put their trust in Christ, God's love is lavished on them. For those who refuse to believe in Jesus Christ, God's wrath abides on them and will be fully displayed on the Day of Judgment. So, let us not get the idea that God's love is shed on all people, believers and unbelievers alike.

John 3:18: *He that believeth on him is not condemned: but he that believeth not is condemned already, because he hath not believed in the name of the only begotten Son of God.*

The love of God is not the kind of love that bypasses sin. His love is not like our love. For example, some parents don't want to chastise their kids with the rod because they think they are demonstrating love by bypassing punishment. With God, it is not so. God will use the rod to chastise His children to keep them on the path of righteousness.

God will not allow His children to continue in sin. He promised to lead them in the path of righteousness for His name's sake. Sin brings death, and God wants us to have eternal life, not eternal death. By Him directing our path into the way of holiness through the chastisement of the rod, His love is demonstrated.

God hates sin, and that's why He created hell and the eternal lake of fire to put an end to it forever.

The Bible constantly declares that God is holy. The angels don't sing about the love of God; they sing about His holiness.

Isaiah 6:3: *And one cried unto another, and said, Holy, holy, holy, is the LORD of hosts: the whole earth is full of his glory.*

Revelation 4:8: *And the four beasts had each of them six wings about him; and they were full of eyes within: and they rest not day and night, saying, Holy, holy, holy, Lord God Almighty, which was, and is, and is to come.*

God says His name is holy. He does not want it to be polluted. Underestimating the holiness of God, as revealed in the Law and Prophets, brings profanity to His name. We are to understand that God is holy! The holy name of God is the most widely stated attribute in Scriptures, not love.

Ezekiel 36:22: *Therefore say unto the house of Israel, Thus saith the Lord GOD; I do not this for your sakes, O house of Israel, but for mine holy name's sake, which ye have profaned among the heathen, whither ye went.*

Ezekiel 39:7: *So will I make my holy name known in the midst of my people Israel; and I will not let them pollute my holy name any more: and the heathen shall know that I am the LORD, the Holy One in Israel.*

Isaiah 57:15: *For thus saith the high and lofty One that inhabiteth eternity, whose name is Holy; I dwell in the high and holy place, with him also that is of a contrite and humble spirit, to revive the spirit of the humble, and to revive the heart of the contrite ones.*

Deuteronomy 32:4: *He is the Rock, his work is perfect: for all his ways are judgment: a God of truth and without iniquity, just and right is he.*

As the Scriptures reveal, God wants us to know that His name is holy and not to be profaned. He is repeatedly referred to in Scriptures as the Holy One. He wants us to be very aware of the fact, that above every other attribute, His holiness has the preeminence.

The saints of the Old and New Testaments also were very aware that God is pure and holy. For example, the Virgin Mary exalted the Lord God and mentioned that His name is holy.

Luke 1:49: *For he that is mighty hath done to me great things; and holy is his name.*

In the Old Testament, Hannah, the mother of the prophet Samuel, and the men of Beth-Shemesh, all testified that the Lord God is holy.

1 Samuel 2:2: *There is none holy as the LORD: for there is none beside thee: neither is there any rock like our God.*

Also, the men of Beth-Shemesh looked into the ark of the Lord, and 50,070 men were struck dead (1 Samuel 6:19). The people lamented greatly because of the great slaughter that the Holy Lord God of Israel had carried out. Great fear came upon them and they exalted God as holy as no other.

1 Samuel 6:20: *And the men of Beth-shemesh said, Who is able to stand before this holy LORD God? and to whom shall he go up from us?*

Consider that three times in Psalm 99, we are reminded that God is holy. We are also told in other Psalms to bless, praise, and exalt the holy name of the Lord.

Psalm 99:3: *Let them praise thy great and terrible name; for it is holy.*

Psalm 99:5: *Exalt ye the LORD our God, and worship at his footstool; for he is holy.*

Psalm 99:9: *Exalt the LORD our God, and worship at his holy hill; for the LORD our God is holy.*

Psalm 103:1: *Bless the LORD, O my soul: and all that is within me, bless his holy name.*

The reason why we are repeatedly told of the holiness of God is to warn us that God is totally against sin. The love of God cannot be displayed on people who delight in sin. It is only displayed after the blood of Christ has washed those sins away.

Sin demands punishment. As the Bible declares, the fruit of sin is death. Therefore, God's justice against sin must be carried out because of His holiness. The Bible describes certain attributes of God like wrath, vengeance, mercy, longsuffering, grace, justice, jealousy, righteousness, and perfection in all His ways.

All these attributes of God are in view of His holiness. For example, God is righteous because He will do what is right according to His perfect holiness.

God is holy and is against sin. God is a God of justice and judgment because sin deserves death. God is also a God of mercy because the death penalty that sinners are supposed to pay for their sins has been transferred to Jesus Christ on the cross.

God has demonstrated His mercy by providing a sacrifice to take the death penalty of the sinner, thereby allowing the sinner to live through the life of the sacrifice. That just and perfect sacrifice was Jesus Christ.

CHAPTER 3

JESUS IS THE RIGHTEOUSNESS OF GOD AND THE END OF THE LAW

Through the cross, God's holiness is maintained as well as His justice, love, and mercy.

As stated in **Romans 1:17**, Jesus is the righteousness of God revealed from heaven. Since Jesus, the Son of God, was as holy as God the Father, He was the only One who could fully satisfy God's throne of holiness and righteousness.

Romans 1:16–17: *For I am not ashamed of the gospel of Christ: for it is the power of God unto salvation to every one that believeth; to the Jew first, and also to the Greek. For therein is the righteousness of God revealed from faith to faith: as it is written, The just shall live by faith.*

Romans 3:25–26: *Whom God hath set forth to be a propitiation through faith in his blood, to declare his righteousness for the remission of sins that are past, through the forbearance of God; To declare, I say, at this time his righteousness: that he might be just, and the justifier of him which believeth in Jesus.*

2 Corinthians 5:21: *For he hath made him to be sin for us, who knew no sin; that we might be made the righteousness of God in him.*

So, we see here in these Scriptures, that Jesus is the only acceptable way to God, Who alone can justify all of humanity as righteous. He does this by giving those who believe in Him His own righteousness, which is called "the righteousness of God".

God the Father has given all things to His only beloved Son and will gladly welcome into His kingdom all who believe and put their trust in Him. It is only through the Son that God's true, perfect righteousness can be imputed to sinners. It is the only way that a person can come to know God and be at peace with Him. No other way is accepted, no matter how sincere one might be in their religious activities. God is not well-pleased with religious activities; On the contrary, He is very angry.

But many have rejected the only righteousness of God revealed in Jesus Christ and have trusted in their own righteousness, which God already condemned as filthy rags in **Isaiah 64:6.** For example, the book of **Romans** tells us that Israel, being ignorant of God's righteousness, has not submitted to the righteousness of God, which is only in Jesus Christ. For this cause, they stumbled at the stumbling stone.

And not only the Israelites, all who refuse to come to Christ for salvation demonstrate their disobedience in submitting to God's true righteousness. The reason is that many still misunderstand or fail to accept God's holy nature, and have made gods in their own likeness—corruptible gods. As the Apostle Paul states about his brethren, the Israelites:

Romans 10:1–4: *Brethren, my heart's desire and prayer to God for Israel is, that they might be saved. For I bear them record that they have a zeal of God, but not according to knowledge. For they being ignorant of God's righteousness, and going about to establish their own righteousness, have not submitted themselves unto the righteousness of God. For Christ is the end of the law for righteousness to every one that believeth.*

Just as the Israelites have gone about establishing their own righteousness, most of the world's population has also not understood the holiness and righteousness of God, and are still trying to please God by their own works.

Jesus himself told the people during His earthly ministry, that unless their righteousness exceeds the righteousness of the Pharisees, they would not enter heaven. In other words, the Pharisees were very religious in keeping the Law, but Jesus said that they could not enter heaven that way.

Matthew 5:20: *For I say unto you, That except your righteousness shall exceed the righteousness of the scribes and Pharisees, ye shall in no case enter into the kingdom of heaven.*

Paul the Apostle was also zealous for the Law, and did not understand the holiness and righteousness of God, until Jesus saved Him, opened his eyes to God's true holiness, and gave Him the Holy Spirit, the Spirit of holiness. Now, Paul's desire was to seek after the righteousness of God, which is only in Jesus Christ, and not his own man-made self-righteousness, which was of the Law.

Philippians 3:7–9: *But what things were gain to me, those I counted loss for Christ. Yea doubtless, and I count all things but loss for the excellency of the knowledge of Christ Jesus my Lord: for whom I have suffered the loss of all things, and do count them but dung, that I may win Christ, And be found in him, not having mine own righteousness, which is of the law, but that which is through the faith of Christ, the righteousness which is of God by faith.*

Romans 3:21–22: *But now the righteousness of God without the law is manifested, being witnessed by the law and the prophets; Even the righteousness of God which is by faith of Jesus Christ unto all and upon all them that believe: for there is no difference.*

Titus 3:5–7: *Not by works of righteousness which we have done, but according to his mercy he saved us, by the washing of regeneration, and renewing of the Holy Ghost. Which he shed on us abundantly through Jesus Christ our Saviour; That being justified by his grace, we should be made heirs according to the hope of eternal life.*

1 Peter 2:24: *Who his own self bare our sins in his own body on the tree, that we, being dead to sins, should live unto righteousness: by whose stripes ye were healed.*

As the Apostle Paul states, he too misunderstood the Law and Prophets, and was also trusting in his own self-righteousness, which comes through Law-keeping. He now understood that the Law and Prophets pointed to the true righteousness of God, which is only in Jesus Christ through faith.

Unfortunately, many today still have a veil over their faces when the Law is read. They still think that the Law of Moses can save them, and have also misunderstood the reason why it was given: to point us to the grace of God in Christ.

2 Corinthians 3:12–14: *Seeing then that we have such hope, we use great plainness of speech: And not as Moses, which put a vail over his face, that the children of Israel could not stedfastly look to the end of that which is abolished: But their minds were blinded: for until this day remaineth the same vail untaken away in the reading of the Old Testament; which vail is done away in Christ.*

As the Apostle Paul addressed this issue of the Law, he says that there is a veil on the hearts of people still to this day, whenever they read the Old Testament, thinking that the keeping of the Law is the way of salvation. They don't seem to understand that Christ fulfilled everything written in the Law and that salvation is not by works of the Law, but by faith in Jesus Christ.

Why is this so? **Galatians 3:24** tells us that the Law was our schoolmaster to bring us to Christ; it's main purpose was to point us to Christ. Jesus also confirmed this truth by stating that the Law and prophets testify of Him as the giver of eternal life, and that he would be crucified and raised from the dead to fulfill that promise.

Acts 10:43: *To him give all the prophets witness, that through his name whosoever believeth in him shall receive remission of sins.*

Galatians 3:24: *Wherefore the law was our schoolmaster to bring us unto Christ, that we might be justified by faith.*

After His resurrection, Jesus expounded the Scriptures to some of His disciples, showing that it was necessary for Him to suffer and rise from the dead, and that repentance and remission of sins should be preached in His name, beginning at Jerusalem.

Luke 24:25–27: *Then he said unto them, O fools, and slow of heart to believe all that the prophets have spoken: Ought not Christ to have suffered these things, and to enter into his glory? And beginning at Moses and all the prophets, he expounded unto them in all the scriptures the things concerning himself.*

Now, all we must do is repent, believe in Him, and follow Him. Why would you ever want to keep the Law if the purpose of the Law was to point us all to Christ, the One spoken of in all Scriptures that would come and fulfill the Law for us and then impute to us His own righteousness as a gift?

CHAPTER 4

REJECTION OF THE TRUE GOSPEL AND REAL JESUS

Why are there so many different interpretations of the gospel?

Since many have rejected the truth of Scriptures and refuse to come to Christ as the only means of salvation, they have come up with various interpretations of Scriptures to justify their own self-righteousness and wickedness. They do this because of their defiled conscience. They have hardened their hearts against the truth of the gospel and now their conscience is defiled. Thus, deception becomes truth and truth becomes a lie.

Because of the rejection of the truth, many have now come up with different interpretations of the Bible, but it is not what God intended. There is only one gospel and one clear meaning. It is not of private personal interpretation.

The Bible tells us that we are joined by the Holy Spirit in one mind, striving for the sake of the gospel (**Phil. 1:27**). How then can there be many interpretations and personal beliefs about what the gospel is, if the Holy Spirit is the Spirit of absolute truth and unity and is the One who reveals the one true gospel message given in Scriptures?

The Bible warns us that not everyone who calls himself a Christian is a true disciple of Christ. This means many so-called "Christians" don't have the Holy Spirit. Those who don't have the Holy Spirit of truth cannot know what the truth is, and they are the ones who have so many different opinions and interpretations of the true gospel.

The Bible also says that all Christians who are truly saved have been born again of the Holy Spirit. Thus, they all have the mind of Christ and know the truth as revealed by the Holy Spirit, the Spirit of truth. You can't convince someone who is sealed by the Holy Spirit that there are other ways to be saved. They know Jesus is the only way because that's a revelation of the Holy Spirit. (That's the reason God gives the Holy Spirit to all who are saved, so that there will be no confusion or division when it comes to the gospel of Christ.)

Anyone not born again of the Spirit does not know God and therefore does not know the truth. The Holy Spirit is the Spirit of God and is called the "Spirit of Truth". All the various gospels bear witness to the fact that these individuals who don't conform to the true gospel, don't know God, and are just following their own sinful ways and performing the work of the Devil (antichrists).

If they had been born of the Holy Spirit, they would know the truth. They would know that the gospel is simple and straightforward as declared in the Old and New Testament Scriptures: Jesus died, was buried, and was raised again for our justification, and that He is the only way to heaven.

The Bible warns us that anyone not preaching the true gospel has a sensual spirit, a demonic spirit, not the Holy Spirit. They are deceivers. They lie in wait to deceive men with their sensual speeches, but are wolves in sheep clothing. For this cause, they are reserved for everlasting destruction if they don't repent and believe the true gospel.

The book of **Jude** was written to warn us of this very thing:

Jude 1:17–19: *But, beloved, remember ye the words which were spoken before of the apostles of our Lord Jesus Christ; How that they told you there should be mockers in the last time, who should walk after their own ungodly lusts. These be they who separate themselves, sensual, having not the Spirit.*

The gospel is a stumbling block to many because it is simple, yet is called the great mystery of God. The sacrifice of Jesus is not like what most people might believe. We have all heard how Jesus died to pay for the sins of the world, but have not fully understood the significance of the cross.

The Bible tells us that the blood of Jesus is not the blood of a regular sinful man like us, but the blood of the Son of God, the new Adam created in true righteousness and holiness. He is the Lord from heaven who came down and was made into the likeness of men, simply to give His life for the sins of the world. He paid for the sins of the people of God—those chosen in Him before the foundation of the world.

Philippians 2:5–8: *Let this mind be in you, which was also in Christ Jesus: Who, being in the form of God, thought it not robbery to be equal with God: But made himself of no reputation, and took upon him the form of a servant, and was made in the likeness of men: And being found in fashion as a man, he humbled himself, and became obedient unto death, even the death of the cross.*

1 John 3:16: *Hereby perceive we the love of God, because he laid down his life for us: and we ought to lay down our lives for the brethren.*

2 Corinthians 5:19: *To wit, that God was in Christ, reconciling the world unto himself, not imputing their trespasses unto them; and hath committed unto us the word of reconciliation.*

Titus 2:13: *Looking for that blessed hope, and the glorious appearing of the great God and our Saviour Jesus Christ.*

2 Peter 1:1: *Simon Peter, a servant and an apostle of Jesus Christ, to them that have obtained like precious faith with us through the righteousness of God and our Saviour Jesus Christ.*

Jude 1:25: *To the only wise God our Saviour, be glory and majesty, dominion and power, both now and ever. Amen.*

1 John 5:20: *And we know that the Son of God is come, and hath given us an understanding, that we may know him that is true, and we are in him that is true, even in his Son Jesus Christ. This is the true God, and eternal life.*

All throughout the New Testament we see the repeated reference to the blood of Jesus Christ. We get the sense that the theme of salvation is all about the atonement that was made for our sins through the blood of

Christ, and that it is the only necessary and vital way that we could ever be forgiven of sins.

We are told in the book of Hebrews that the blood of bulls and goats could not make the people offering those sacrifices perfect as pertaining to their conscience. In contrast, what the blood of Jesus does is purge the conscience of sin—something that is unique to the gospel.

Under the Old Testament, the blood of animals purified only the flesh, but could not take away sins. But now, the blood of Christ is the only thing that can purge the conscience of sins and bring peace with God to all who believe and receive it. There is nothing else in the world that can do this!

Jesus is the Lord God Almighty in human flesh.

The gospel message declaring that Jesus is the True and Eternal God is called the great mystery of God, which cannot be explained by human wisdom, but the Bible, with its numerous prophecies already fulfilled, firmly authenticate this claim and confirms truly that Jesus Christ is God in human flesh, called the Son of God.

The subject of Jesus being the Son of God has always been a topic that causes debates and divisions. Too many cannot understand how it is possible for Jesus to be Son of God. They claim that God does not have a Son, because that's not possible. They say it's just ridiculous and blasphemous.

They forget that this mystery is not something that we can conceive. The Bible tells us in the book of **Job** that God does things which no one can understand.

Job 37:5: *God thundereth marvellously with his voice; great things doeth he, which we cannot comprehend.*

Other Scriptures also tell us that there is none like God, and that's why He should be greatly feared. This great mystery that God was in Christ reconciling the world unto Himself is a fact we cannot comprehend.

The Scriptures constantly declare that Jesus is God the Creator in a body. This is truly hard to believe, but it's true. It is clearly stated here in **1 Timothy 3:16:**

And without controversy great is the mystery of godliness: God was manifest in the flesh, justified in the Spirit, seen of angels, preached unto the Gentiles, believed on in the world, received up into glory.

Colossians 1:26–27: *Even the mystery which hath been hid from ages and from generations, but now is made manifest to his saints: To whom God would make known what is the riches of the glory of this mystery among the Gentiles; which is Christ in you, the hope of glory:*

Ephesians 3:9: *And to make all men see what is the fellowship of the mystery, which from the beginning of the world hath been hid in God, who created all things by Jesus Christ.*

This mystery of Christ as being God in human flesh is what many people stumble on. They cannot understand how it is conceivable that Jesus is God, but that's exactly what the Bible says, "Great is the mystery of godliness: God was manifest in the flesh".

The Bible does not say that it is a simple mystery, but a great one. Now, how are you going to explain a great mystery? What do you think a mystery is? Of course, it's unexplainable, like miracles.

The blood of Jesus Christ is the only payment for sins.

The blood of Christ paid for the sins of those under the Old Testament covenant (first testament) and is more than sufficient for all past, present, and future generations.

Many might wonder about those people who were under the Old Testament covenant whether they were forgiven of their sins apart from the blood of Christ. What is amazing about the cross is that Jesus also paid for their sins, which were transferred to Him on the cross. Through

His sacrifice, all the saints of the Old Testament who were already justified by faith as righteous could not have had remission of their sins, receive their new immortal body, or enter heaven without the death, burial, and resurrection of Christ.

This verse from the book of Hebrews speaks to this issue of the sins of the Old Testament saints being paid for by Christ when they were transferred from the old covenant.

Hebrews 9:13–15: *For if the blood of bulls and of goats, and the ashes of an heifer sprinkling the unclean, sanctifieth to the purifying of the flesh: How much more shall the blood of Christ, who through the eternal Spirit offered himself without spot to God, purge your conscience from dead works to serve the living God? And for this cause he is the mediator of the New Testament, that by means of death, for the redemption of the transgressions that were under the first testament, they which are called might receive the promise of eternal inheritance.*

Romans 3:23–25: *For all have sinned, and come short of the glory of God; Being justified freely by his grace through the redemption that is in Christ Jesus: Whom God hath set forth to be a propitiation through faith in his blood, to declare his righteousness for the remission of sins that are past, through the forbearance of God.*

Essentially, the gospel shows that Jesus is the One the Holy Scriptures declares to grant forgiveness of sins for all people through His sacrifice, from Adam to the end of all ages. Everything resides in Him, no matter if you were two thousand years back in the Old Testament looking forward to the cross, or two thousand years forward looking back to the cross.

The Bible reveals Jesus as God.

Very essential to the gospel is the deity of the Lord Jesus Christ. It is very important to know that Jesus is God, and that all things are under Him. He is God our Savior. As He delivered the children of Israel from the bondage of Pharaoh in Egypt, He also came and delivered us from the bondage of sin through His own death, burial, and resurrection, by putting on a body.

In other words, He was manifested in the flesh—God made visible in human form. All power in heaven and earth is in His hands. The breath of all mankind is in His hands. This is the main part of the gospel that causes many to stumble and reject the true gospel, and embrace a false one that denies Jesus as God. Jesus did not say He was a good teacher or just a prophet of God, as many false gospels and other religions are proclaiming.

Why would we preach salvation is only in Jesus Christ and lose our lives doing it, if Jesus were not God?

Since Jesus is revealed to be the Only True and Eternal God, He is obviously the Creator of all things, as the Bible also strongly declares:

Colossians 1:15–17: *Who is the image of the invisible God, the firstborn of every creature: For by him were all things created, that are in heaven, and that are in earth, visible and invisible, whether they be thrones, or dominions, or principalities, or powers: all things were created by him, and for him: And he is before all things, and by him all things consist.*

Hebrews 1:1–3: *God, who at sundry times and in divers manners spake in time past unto the fathers by the prophets, Hath in these last days spoken unto us by his Son, whom he hath appointed heir of all things, by whom also he made the worlds; Who being the brightness of his glory, and the express image of his person, and upholding all things by the word of his power, when he had by himself purged our sins, sat down on the right hand of the Majesty on high.*

Revelation 4:11: *Thou art worthy, O Lord, to receive glory and honour and power: for thou hast created all things, and for thy pleasure they are and were created.*

The Bible strongly declares that Jesus is God, Christ the Lord, who took the form of human likeness, and died on the cross to pay for our sins Himself. For this reason, He is proclaimed to be the only Savior and hope for the world. It is obvious that since He is God, He controls all things, including salvation.

You must know that Jesus is the Lord God Almighty. You cannot miss this part. Everything hangs on this foundation. Jesus only builds His church on the confession that He is the Son of God: God in human flesh.

The angels declared this truth to the shepherds the night the Lord Jesus took on human flesh (the night He came into this world):

Luke 2:11: *For unto you is born this day in the city of David a Saviour, which is Christ the Lord.*

Do you hear what the angels proclaimed to the shepherds? They said "today is born in the city of David, a Savior, which is Christ the Lord. They told the shepherds that the Savior is Christ the Lord. Jesus is Lord and the Lord is God. Do you get it? Jesus is God.

1 Timothy 1:1: *Paul, an apostle of Jesus Christ by the commandment of God our Saviour, and Lord Jesus Christ, which is our hope.*

Acts 4:12: *Neither is there salvation in any other: for there is none other name under heaven given among men, whereby we must be saved.*

John 4:42: *And said unto the woman, Now we believe, not because of thy saying: for we have heard him ourselves, and know that this is indeed the Christ, the Saviour of the world.*

CHAPTER 5

JESUS CREATED AND RULES OVER EVERYTHING IN THE UNIVERSE: VISIBLE AND INVISIBLE

So many people assume that if you believe in God and practice your own religion, then God will accept it. That's not true. Everyone must come through Jesus to get to heaven. The Bible also tells us that there are many lords and gods, but only One True Eternal God and Lord who is above them all, Jesus Christ.

This phrase "many lords and gods" is evident in Hinduism, Buddhism, Islam, and so many other "isms", where they worship millions of gods. Nevertheless, although there are many religions in the world that don't recognize Jesus as the Lord God Almighty, they will still have to give an account to Him on the Day of Judgment, because He is the Judge of both the living and the dead.

This means that all people who believe they must stand before God on judgment day will stand before the Son of God, the Lord Jesus Christ.

As declared in this passage of the Bible:

1 Corinthians 8:5–6: *For though there be that are called gods, whether in heaven or in earth, (as there be gods many, and lords many,) But to us there is but one God, the Father, of whom are all things, and we in him; and one Lord Jesus Christ, by whom are all things, and we by him.*

What about other religions that don't believe Jesus is the only Savior?

Since Jesus is The Eternal God, this means that all people must go through Him to be saved. As already stated, there are many lords and gods in the world, but Jesus is the King of kings, and Lord of lords. For this reason, He is the only Savior and source of eternal life for those who want to live forever in heaven.

Religions deceive people in promising them eternal life if they follow their prescribed standards, but that won't give them eternal life. These standards are usually based on certain deeds one must perform to please God and thereby qualify for entry into heaven.

God is the source of eternal life. When Jesus (God) came, He came to give us that eternal life as a gift, not something we work for. We didn't give ourselves the breath of life to begin with, so how do we expect to work for eternal life by doing good deeds? Eternal life is a gift from God.

Jesus is the One who gives eternal life. Doing good deeds is only a deception of self-righteousness, but the reality remains that Jesus is the only source of eternal life, and without coming to Him for it, there is no other way to obtain it.

The Bible reveals Jesus Christ as the eternal King over all kings and eternal Lord over all lords: the only source of eternal life.

The Bible shows that Jesus is God the King, who is exalted above all kings and gods, whose kingdom rules over all.

Revelation 19:16: *And he hath on his vesture and on his thigh a name written, KING OF KINGS, AND LORD OF LORDS.*

John 6:47: *Verily, verily, I say unto you, He that believeth on me hath everlasting life.*

Mark 16:16: *He that believeth and is baptized shall be saved; but he that believeth not shall be damned.*

John 3:36: *He that believeth on the Son hath everlasting life: and he that believeth not the Son shall not see life; but the wrath of God abideth on him.*

Acts 10:43: *To him give all the prophets witness, that through his name whosoever believeth in him shall receive remission of sins.*

Acts 13:39: *And by him all that believe are justified from all things, from which ye could not be justified by the law of Moses.*

Plainly stated, all who trust in their religion or their good deeds, and will not come to Jesus Christ to receive remission of sins, cannot enter heaven. In this case, the wrath of God abides on them and eternal punishment is the consequence.

Jesus warned the Pharisees and those who trust in their good deeds or religious activities, that they must come to Him to have eternal life. If not, they will be condemned to everlasting fire. Jesus is God and has all authority and right to make this statement, because it is the truth.

John 5:39–40: *Search the scriptures; for in them ye think ye have eternal life: and they are they which testify of me. And ye will not come to me, that ye might have life.*

John 3:18: *He that believeth on him is not condemned: but he that believeth not is condemned already, because he hath not believed in the name of the only begotten Son of God.*

This warning is for every person on this planet. This does not exclude anyone. This warning is for all of humanity without exception. It doesn't matter if you are a Jew or Gentile, Muslim, Buddhist, so-called Christian but not born again, and all other religious persons. Everyone must come to Jesus and be saved; there is no other way to get to heaven.

I know many of the religious world don't want to hear this gospel, but they will perish in the lake of fire for not believing it. I know they want to believe that their religion or religious activities can save them. But absolute truth is absolute truth whether people want to believe it or not.

Shall unbelief change the fact that Jesus is the only way to be forgiven of sins and enter heaven? Can the belief by atheists that there is no God change the fact that there is a God who is so great and mighty that we cannot comprehend His majesty? I think not.

God exists whether we believe or not. Jesus is God the only Savior whether some believe it or not. The Bible proves that, not just in words to be taken by blind faith, but with infallible proofs demonstrated through the fulfillment of numerous prophecies.

Rejecting Jesus as the Son of God and Savior of the world makes God a liar.

Not believing that Jesus is the Savior of the world and Son of God makes God a liar, which is a very serious charge. As we all know, God is True and Faithful, and Satan is the liar. For this reason, not believing in Jesus tells God He is a liar as the Devil. Thus, eternal punishment is the reward for rejecting the blood of Christ, and not believing He is the Son of God.

1 John 5:10: *He that believeth on the Son of God hath the witness in himself: he that believeth not God hath made him a liar; because he believeth not the record that God gave of his Son.*

1 John 5:7–8: *For there are three that bear record in heaven, the Father, the Word, and the Holy Ghost: and these three are one. And there are three that bear witness in earth, the Spirit, and the water, and the blood: and these three agree in one.*

So certain is the message of the gospel of Christ as the only means of salvation, that God has recorded it in heaven and earth. The Holy Spirit bears witness of Christ both in heaven and on the earth. Consequently, anyone who does not believe in the Son of God is under eternal damnation.

The Bible has proven itself to be the infallible Word of God and is trustworthy. The many prophecies fulfilled exactly as stated already demonstrate the inerrancy of the Bible as God's Word. Whatever is written are the actual words of the Eternal God.

Wherever it states that Jesus is the Son of God, that is the very absolute truth of God. This statement is so certain that God says that anyone who does not believe it makes Him a liar. Referring to God as a liar and not repenting through the blood of Jesus Christ carries eternal judgment.

The gospel declares that there is absolutely no other way to enter heaven but through Jesus Christ!

Since Jesus is declared to be the Creator of all things in the universe, whatever He says stands. If He says that He is the only way to heaven, then that is the absolute truth. He restates this even more clearly by saying that if anyone tries to enter heaven any other way than through Him (the door), that person is a thief. I hope we all know that thieves cannot enter heaven.

John 10:9: *I am the door: by me if any man enter in, he shall be saved, and shall go in and out, and find pasture.*

John 10:1: *Verily, verily, I say unto you, He that entereth not by the door into the sheepfold, but climbeth up some other way, the same is a thief and a robber.*

John 14:6: *Jesus saith unto him, I am the way, the truth, and the life: no man cometh unto the Father, but by me.*

You cannot be confused with this truth. It is so clearly stated by Jesus that you cannot get to heaven any other way but through Him. Whatever religion you are trusting in to save you, that will not work. Your religion is exactly like a thief trying to climb over the door to get into heaven. You can't climb over the door; you must come through the door: Jesus.

Jesus is the Great High Priest.

Another compelling reason why Jesus is the only way to be saved is because of His eternal, unchangeable priesthood.

The Bible tells us that high priests were chosen by God to offer gifts and sacrifices for sins. These high priests were ordained under the Law of the Levitical priesthood (of the tribe of Levi). They were ordained by God to stand and minister before God on behalf of the people. In other words, they spoke to God for the people.

Hebrews 5:1: *For every high priest taken from among men is ordained for men in things pertaining to God, that he may offer both gifts and sacrifices for sins.*

Since these high priests were also sinners, they had to offer sacrifices first for their own sins, and then for the sins of the people. Moreover, they had to be constantly replaced due to death. For these reasons, God made a promise that He would ordain His own High Priest who would stand in His very presence to minister for the people, and that the promised High Priest would have an eternal priesthood.

***Hebrews 4:14**: Seeing then that we have a great high priest, that is passed into the heavens, Jesus the Son of God, let us hold fast our profession.*

***Hebrews 5:5:** So also Christ glorified not himself to be made an high priest; but he that said unto him, Thou art my Son, today have I begotten thee.*

We see that Jesus was made the Great High Priest whose priesthood is eternal and who was made higher than the heavens. He stands at the right hand of God the Father and continually makes intercession. For this reason, He can save to the very end all that come through Him.

First, Jesus the Great High Priest is sinless, meaning He does not have to offer sacrifices for His own sins before interceding for sinners. In this sense, He is far superior than previous high priests.

Secondly, He sits at the right hand of God on the throne in heaven. This was no way the case of previous high priests. They could only appear once a year into the holy of holies and they could not sit (**Exodus 30:10**). Through Jesus, we can now come to God any time, any second, any minute, hour, and day.

Thirdly, Jesus is eternal. This means His priesthood is unchangeable and will never be replaced. He is able, without fail, to save sinners, not only because of His priesthood, but also because of the sacrifice He offered for sins: His own blood. Now, that's truly a Great High Priest who can save sinners!

***Hebrews 7:24–25:** But this man, because he continueth ever, hath an unchangeable priesthood. Wherefore he is able also to save them to the uttermost that* *come unto God by him, seeing he ever liveth to make intercession for them.*

Jesus is the Judge of the world.

Why does the Bible say that all must go through Jesus to be saved?

Not only is Jesus the only Savior of the world, He is also the only Judge. If the religious world knew this, they would understand why the Bible declares Him to be the only way to be saved. If Jesus were not the Judge on the Day of Judgment, then people might seem to have some valid excuse on that terrible day why they didn't accept Him as Lord and Savior.

Unfortunately, just when the religious thought their religion would save them, they now stand before Christ, the Judge of all the living and the dead. I'm sorry to say this, but it will be very tragic and most terrifying! No excuse can save them now, because it is the Day of Judgment; mercy would have already been ended.

The Bible tells us that Jesus is the True and Eternal God in human form (**1 Timothy 3:16**). For this reason, He is also the Judge of all people on the Day of Judgment. Everyone must face Him after death!

Although people of various religions, including Islam, also believe in the second coming of Christ, they don't understand the truth of it. The reason why He is coming back, as many have already heard, is to judge the world for rejecting Him, and to reward those who believe in Him.

John 5:22–23: *For the Father judgeth no man, but hath committed all judgment unto the Son: That all men should honour the Son, even as they honour the Father. He that honoureth not the Son honoureth not the Father which hath sent him.*

John 12:48: *He that rejecteth me, and receiveth not my words, hath one that judgeth him: the word that I have spoken, the same shall judge him in the last day.*

Acts 10:42: *And he commanded us to preach unto the people, and to testify that it is he which was ordained of God to be the Judge of quick and dead.*

Romans 2:16: *In the day when God shall judge the secrets of men by Jesus Christ according to my gospel.*

Romans 14:10: *But why dost thou judge thy brother? or why dost thou set at nought thy brother? for we shall all stand before the judgment seat of Christ.*

2 Timothy 4:1: *I charge thee therefore before God, and the Lord Jesus Christ, who shall judge the quick and the dead at his appearing and his kingdom.*

Revelation 19:11: *And I saw heaven opened, and behold a white horse; and he that sat upon him was called Faithful and True, and in righteousness he doth judge and make war.*

2 Corinthians 5:10: *For we must all appear before the judgment seat of Christ; that every one may receive the things done in his body, according to that he hath done, whether it be good or bad.*

So many Scriptures constantly restate the truth that Jesus is the Judge of the world. To be sure you can face the Judge with confidence, why not do what He has commanded you to do now: repent and believe in Him to be saved? What will you tell Him on Judgment Day, that you didn't hear the true gospel I am declaring to you now?

Jesus is also the King of Heaven.

Another surprise for those who reject Christ and wish to enter heaven is the fact that Jesus is also the King who rules in heaven. Jesus is the King of heaven and earth. If you don't do what the King says, how do you expect to get into His kingdom? That's another reason why all who want to enter heaven must go through Him.

Why would you want to be in heaven if you despise the King of heaven? Does it make any sense for anyone to live in peace in the splendor and glories of heaven when they hate the Ruler of heaven? If you have not made peace with the King, how can you live at peace with Him in His kingdom?

To make peace with the King, you must recognize the authority of the

King. Accept Him and believe in what He says you must do to be a part of His kingdom. Confess your sins to Him and accept the blood of His cross as the only way to make peace with Him, and the only way by which you can enter heaven. This is what the King says.

John 18:36: *Jesus answered, My kingdom is not of this world: if my kingdom were of this world, then would my servants fight, that I should not be delivered to the Jews: but now is my kingdom not from hence.*

Revelation 19:16: *And he hath on his vesture and on his thigh a name written, KING OF KINGS, AND LORD OF LORDS.*

Matthew 25:34: *Then shall the King say unto them on his right hand, Come, ye blessed of my Father, inherit the kingdom prepared for you from the foundation of the world.*

Matthew 27:37: *And set up over his head his accusation written, THIS IS JESUS THE KING OF THE JEWS.*

The gospel must be preached to the four corners of the earth before Christ returns.

Jesus has promised that the gospel would be preached all over the world before He returns. He wants everyone to hear the message so that they may repent and believe in Him to escape the wrath of God. It is not His will than anyone should perish eternally in hell for their sins when He has already paid the price so they don't have to.

Even though many reject the gospel message and would rather not hear it, it will still be proclaimed as promised. For over 2000 years, many have tried to stop the gospel message, but have been unsuccessful. Jesus already said that the gospel would be preached throughout the entire world to all nations as a witness, and that statement was not a wish, but an order from the King of Kings.

Let me say it this way: whatever Jesus says will take place, must happen. He made this statement in ***Luke 21:33:*** *Heaven and earth shall pass away:*

but my words shall not pass away.

Isn't the gospel still being preached today to prove that what Jesus said in the Bible must take place because He is the Eternal God and Savior? He has full sovereignty over all things, including the proclamation of His gospel message to the four corners of the earth, and no one will ever stop it!

Matthew: 24:14: *And this gospel of the kingdom shall be preached in all the world for a witness unto all nations; and then shall the end come.*

Mark 13:10: *And the gospel must first be published among all nations.*

Mark 16:15: *And he said unto them, Go ye into all the world, and preach the gospel to every creature.*

It is God's will that all should hear the gospel and repent, because He doesn't want anyone to perish in the eternal lake of fire, but to be forgiven of their sins through the blood of Christ. Even though many have rejected Christ and have despised the gospel, God is still willing to save them, if they will acknowledge their sin and come to Him for mercy.

Most of us don't think about Judgment Day. We forget that one day we will all have to stand before God to give an account of our lives. While we might forget, God does not forget, because He knows exactly how terrible that day will be for those who are not forgiven of their sins. For this reason, God is still waiting for even the worst blasphemers of the name of Christ to come and be saved.

2 Peter 3:9: *The Lord is not slack concerning his promise, as some men count slackness; but is longsuffering to us-ward, not willing that any should perish, but that all should come to repentance.*

1 Timothy 2:4: *Who will have all men to be saved, and to come unto the knowledge of the truth.*

Ezekiel 18:23: *Have I any pleasure at all that the wicked should die? saith the Lord GOD: and not that he should return from his ways, and live?*

The gospel of Christ is very offensive, and many will reject it.

With so many different views of the holiness and righteousness of God, as depicted in the various religions of the world, it is no surprise that the gospel is very offensive. Let's face it, not all people view God the same way. Thus, everyone seems to have a different view when it comes to the subject of salvation (how to be saved from eternal hell and enter heaven).

While the world seems to be broad-minded, the God of the Bible is very narrow-minded on the topic of sin and salvation. He does not compromise; neither will He acquit sinners of their sins apart from faith in Jesus Christ.

The gospel message is very narrow and clear about Jesus being the only way to be saved, and leaves no room for discussion or change, on God's part. Since God already knows the thoughts of man, He warned that many would reject the gospel message and not accept the narrow way.

For those who have rejected the gospel, they have just fulfilled the words of Christ who already forewarned that many in His day, and many more in the present day, would reject him, as we are currently witnessing.

Luke 7:23: *And blessed is he, whosoever shall not be offended in me.*

Luke 17:25: *But first must he suffer many things, and be rejected of this generation.*

Matthew 24:10: *And then shall many be offended, and shall betray one another, and shall hate one another.*

Mark 6:3: *Is not this the carpenter, the son of Mary, the brother of James, and Joses, and of Juda, and Simon? and are not his sisters here with us? And they were offended at him.*

CHAPTER 6

JESUS: THE ONLY RIGHTEOUSNESS OF GOD, WITHOUT THE WORKS OF THE LAW

Why do we need to believe in Jesus in order to enter heaven? Can't we just follow the Law of Moses and God will accept us into heaven?

The Law of Moses is one of the biggest obstacles religious individuals face. They don't seem to understand that the Law was given to prepare us for Christ. It was given to convict the entire world of sin to bring us to the grace of God given in Christ.

In other words, trying to keep the Law does not justify one as righteous, but was a witness to the true righteousness of God, to be fulfilled through the death, burial, and resurrection of Christ.

Galatians 2:21: *I do not frustrate the grace of God: for if righteousness come by the law, then Christ is dead in vain.*

Romans 3:19–20: *Now we know that what things soever the law saith, it saith to them who are under the law: that every mouth may be stopped, and all the world may become guilty before God. Therefore by the deeds of the law there shall no flesh be justified in his sight: for by the law is the knowledge of sin.*

When God gave the Law to Moses, He made it clear that all things written in it must be obeyed perfectly. If anyone breaks the Law, they are cursed by God. In other words, we are not perfect, and we have all broken the Law. That means we are cursed and to be punished.

Deuteronomy 27:26: *Cursed be he that confirmeth not all the words of this law to do them. And all the people shall say, Amen.*

Even though it is clearly stated in the Law of Moses that we are to be perfect, some will try to get around this by saying: "Well, God knows I'm not perfect, so if I break one, He will understand". No, God doesn't understand why you refuse to listen.

Deuteronomy 18:13: *Thou shalt be perfect with the LORD thy God.*

Many forget that Laws are not made for righteous people but for the Lawless and disobedient—criminals. We were given the Law because we were all evil, and God gave it to punish us for our evil. Why are Laws made? Laws don't make criminals saints. They are used to punish evildoers for their evil works.

1 Timothy 1:9: *Knowing this, that the law is not made for a righteous man, but for the lawless and disobedient, for the ungodly and for sinners, for unholy and profane, for murderers of fathers and murderers of mothers, for manslayers…*

The Law of Moses is called the Law of condemnation and death. It was given to convict the world of sin and to reveal Jesus Christ, the Word of God made flesh and the Savior of the world. Jesus already fulfilled the Law for us since none of us has ever perfectly obeyed it. This is what He made known to the religious leaders of His day. The Pharisees were trusting in their Law-keeping religion to save them, but Jesus made it known to them that no one, including them, can keep the Law.

John 7:19: *Did not Moses give you the law, and yet none of you keepeth the Law? Why go ye about to kill me?*

Matthew 5:17: *Think not that I am come to destroy the law, or the prophets: I am not come to destroy, but to fulfil.*

Romans 8:3-4: *For what the law could not do, in that it was weak through the flesh, God sending his own Son in the likeness of sinful flesh, and for sin, condemned sin in the flesh: That the righteousness of the law might be fulfilled in us, who walk not after the flesh, but after the Spirit.*

The Law and Prophets testify of Jesus Christ as the Savior, while condemning all as sinners who cannot in any way of their own, specifically a Law-keeping religion, save themselves. In other words, anyone who measures himself against the Law and thinks he is doing well actually confirms that he is an evildoer worthy of God's eternal punishment.

Why follow the Law if you are already righteous? Didn't you hear what the Apostle Paul said in **1 Timothy 1:9**, that the Law was given for the Lawless and disobedient? Didn't you hear what he also said in the book of **Galatians**, that if righteousness came by the Law, then Christ died in vain? How can you keep the Law while trusting in Christ at the same time? They are in opposite directions.

As declared in the Word of God, all the Scriptures of Moses and the other prophets testify of Jesus as the One through whom remission of sins and eternal life would be granted. For this cause, God cannot justify those who follow the Law of Moses as righteous, because the Law testifies of Christ as the Savior of the world and the righteousness of God. Hence, for anyone to be justified as righteous, faith in Christ alone is the means, without the deeds of the Law.

Galatians 2:16: *Knowing that a man is not justified by the works of the law, but by the faith of Jesus Christ, even we have believed in Jesus Christ, that we might be justified by the faith of Christ, and not by the works of the law: for by the works of the law shall no flesh be justified.*

Galatians 3:24: *Wherefore the law was our schoolmaster to bring us unto Christ, that we might be justified by faith.*

Romans 3:19: *Now we know that what things soever the Law saith, it saith to them who are under the law: that every mouth may be stopped, and all the world may become guilty before God.*

John 5:46: *For had ye believed Moses, ye would have believed me: for he wrote of me.*

Luke 24:27: *And beginning at Moses and all the prophets, he expounded unto them in all the scriptures the things concerning himself.*

Luke 24:44: *And he said unto them, These are the words which I spake unto you, while I was yet with you, that all things must be fulfilled, which were written in the*

Law of Moses, and in the prophets, and in the psalms, concerning me.

John 1:45: *Philip findeth Nathanael, and saith unto him, We have found him, of whom Moses in the law, and the prophets, did write, Jesus of Nazareth, the son of Joseph.*

Acts 10:43: *To him give all the prophets witness, that through his name whosoever believeth in him shall receive remission of sins.*

Acts 13:39: *And by him all that believe are justified from all things, from which ye could not be justified by the law of Moses.*

The Holy Scriptures testify that Jesus is the Lord God who gives salvation.

All the Holy Scriptures speak of Jesus Christ, the Word of God who became flesh. That's another reason why all people must come to Him to be saved. The entire writings of Moses and the prophets speak of Him as the only way of salvation.

John 1:1: *In the beginning was the Word, and the Word was with God, and the Word was God.*

Revelation 19:13: *And he was clothed with a vesture dipped in blood: and his name is called The Word of God.*

Psalm 3:8: *Salvation belongeth unto the LORD: thy blessing is upon thy people. Selah.*

Isaiah 12:2: *Behold, God is my salvation; I will trust, and not be afraid: for the LORD JEHOVAH is my strength and my song; he also is become my salvation.*

Habakkuk 3:18: *Yet I will rejoice in the LORD, I will joy in the God of my salvation.*

Isaiah 25:9: *And it shall be said in that day, Lo, this is our God; we have waited for him, and he will save us: this is the LORD; we have waited for him, we will be glad and rejoice in his salvation.*

The prophets wrote that "the Lord God is my salvation, we have waited for Him and he will save us, and we will rejoice in His salvation". Jesus fulfilled this prophecy when He came to earth as the Lord God of our salvation.

Even though it may not be apparent, all the stories in the Old Testament testify of salvation in Christ. But only through revelation of the Holy Spirit can one come to this knowledge. The stories of Joseph, Noah, Abraham, etc. and so on, all tell the story of the Great God, Lord and Savior, Jesus Christ.

All these stories in the Old Testament of Rebecca, Isaac, Jacob, and others, are shadows of Christ's redemptive work of salvation. You will not be able to understand it until Jesus shows you. Jesus Himself gave this revelation to the disciples, after His resurrection.

Luke 24:36–47: *And as they thus spake, Jesus himself stood in the midst of them, and saith unto them, Peace be unto you. But they were terrified and affrighted, and supposed that they had seen a spirit. And he said unto them, Why are ye troubled? and why do thoughts arise in your hearts? Behold my hands and my feet, that it is I myself: handle me, and see; for a spirit hath not flesh and bones, as ye see me have. And when he had thus spoken, he shewed them his hands and his feet. And while they yet believed not for joy, and wondered, he said unto them, Have ye here any meat? And they gave him a piece of a broiled fish, and of an honeycomb. And he took it, and did eat before them.*

And he said unto them, These are the words which I spake unto you, while I was yet with you, that all things must be fulfilled, which were written in the law of Moses, and in the prophets, and in the psalms, concerning me. Then opened he their understanding, that they might understand the scriptures, And said unto them, Thus it is written, and thus it behoved Christ to suffer, and to rise from the dead the third day: And that repentance and remission of sins should be preached in his name among all nations, beginning at Jerusalem.

CHAPTER 7

ORDINANCES OF THE LAW AND FAITH IN CHRIST

The kingdom of God is not about abstaining from certain meats and drinks nor performing religious ordinances, but is about righteousness, joy, and peace in the Holy Ghost.

Romans 14:17: *For the kingdom of God is not meat and drink; but righteousness, and peace, and joy in the Holy Ghost.*

Another doctrine that is not a part of the saving gospel is regarding dietary restrictions that were imposed by the Law.

These restrictions were imposed until Christ came and fulfilled the Law. We are not under any dietary restrictions as the children of Israel were.

Colossians 2:13–15: *And you, being dead in your sins and the uncircumcision of your flesh, hath he quickened together with him, having forgiven you all trespasses; Blotting out the handwriting of ordinances that was against us, which was contrary to us, and took it out of the way, nailing it to his cross; And having spoiled principalities and powers, he made a shew of them openly, triumphing over them in it.*

Some churches like the Sabbath-keeping churches will say that Jesus commanded us to keep His commandments including Old Testament dietary restrictions, but that's not true. Jesus never said to follow ordinances of the Law as being His new commandments of love. He said, to "love God and your neighbor as yourself are the two main commandments that the Law and the Prophets hang on.

Matthew 22:37–40: *Jesus said unto him, Thou shalt love the Lord thy God with all thy heart, and with all thy soul, and with all thy mind.*

This is the first and great commandment. And the second is like unto it, Thou shalt love thy neighbour as thyself. On these two commandments hang all the law and the prophets.

Whenever Jesus was questioned by religious leaders about the commandments, He always gave love as the answer. He even gave some parables, like the good Samaritan to explain love as the main point of the Law.

He also said in another passage that the Law and Prophets state whatever you would want done to you, do to others.

Matthew 7:12: *Therefore all things whatsoever ye would that men should do to you, do ye even so to them: for this is the law and the prophets.*

The book of Hebrews tells us that carnal ordinances were imposed on the people of God until the time of reformation. That time of reformation came when Christ came and finished the work of salvation. We are warned not to be concerned with strange doctrines, such as abstaining from certain meats and drinks, because that is not profitable to the true essence of the gospel.

Hebrews 9:10: *Which stood only in meats and drinks, and divers washings, and carnal ordinances, imposed on them until the time of reformation.*

Hebrews 13:9: *Be not carried about with divers and strange doctrines. For it is a good thing that the heart be established with grace; not with meats, which have not profited them that have been occupied therein.*

This doctrine regarding the avoidance of certain meats is widely spoken of in the New Testament. We were warned that in the latter times some would teach this doctrine, which is of a seducing spirit, and is a departure from the faith. The doctrine that says we are to abstain from certain meats is not part of the gospel. It only brings confusion to the true gospel, which is the grace of God in Jesus Christ.

Jesus was confronted with this doctrine by the Pharisees, and he said that there is nothing that a man eats that can defile him, but what comes from his heart. Then Jesus said, "Let him who has ears to hear, hear."

Mark 7:15–16: *There is nothing from without a man, that entering into him can defile him: but the things which come out of him, those are they that defile the man. If any man have ears to hear, let him hear.*

It is important to know this truth regarding meat, because many will try to lead the people of God astray with strange or false doctrines, such as abstaining from certain meats, which are not edifying.

For this reason, the Bible clearly tells us not to let anyone judge us regarding meat or Sabbath days.

Colossians 2:16: *Let no man therefore judge you in meat, or in drink, or in respect of an holyday, or of the new moon, or of the sabbath days.*

There were certain animals classified as unclean by the Law, which the children of Israel were not allowed to eat. Now, in the New Testament, after the death, burial, and resurrection of Christ for our sanctification and justification, we see God telling Peter to rise and eat, but Peter would not, because he did not yet understand the meaning of the sacrifice of Christ, as with many today.

In the Old Testament, God said, "You must not eat certain animals", but in the New Testament, He says to Peter "Rise and eat". Is there a contradiction? No. The Bible tells us that those ordinances of the Law were carnal and were just a shadow of what was to come, Jesus Christ. Listen here carefully! Jesus always warns us to listen. He says repeatedly, "Let him who has ears listen to what the Spirit says". The Word of God is Spirit, not human wisdom.

In the Old Testament, the Gentiles were unclean. In the New Testament, they are now sanctified and made clean by Jesus Christ. The blood of Christ and the sanctifying power of the Holy Spirit now make them clean.

In other words, the unclean animals referred to in the Old Testament were pictures of all nations that were not a part of the covenant of God, the Gentiles. Through Jesus Christ, they are now sanctified by His death, burial, and resurrection.

Acts 10:14–15: *But Peter said, Not so, Lord; for I have never eaten anything that is common or unclean. And the voice spake unto him again the second time, What God hath cleansed, that call not thou common.*

Romans 15:16: *That I should be the minister of Jesus Christ to the Gentiles, ministering the gospel of God, that the offering up of the Gentiles might be acceptable, being sanctified by the Holy Ghost.*

The Old Testament Law and sacrificial ordinances were temporary until the Messiah, Jesus Christ, would come to bring about true righteousness by the indwelling power of the Holy Spirit, the Spirit of holiness.

God made a promise that He would make a new covenant which makes the old covenant obsolete.

Hebrews 8:8–13: *For finding fault with them, he saith, Behold, the days come, saith the Lord, when I will make a new covenant with the house of Israel and with the house of Judah: Not according to the covenant that I made with their fathers in the day when I took them by the hand to lead them out of the land of Egypt; because they continued not in my covenant, and I regarded them not, saith the Lord. For this is the covenant that I will make with the house of Israel after those days, saith the Lord; I will put my laws into their mind, and write them in their hearts: and I will be to them a God, and they shall be to me a people: And they shall not teach every man his neighbour, and every man his brother, saying, Know the Lord: for all shall know me, from the least to the greatest. For I will be merciful to their unrighteousness, and their sins and their iniquities will I remember no more. In that he saith, A new covenant, he hath made the first old. Now that which decayeth and waxeth old is ready to vanish away.*

Romans 14:20: *For meat destroy not the work of God. All things indeed are pure; but it is evil for that man who eateth with offence.*

1 Corinthians 8:8: *But meat commendeth us not to God: for neither, if we eat, are we the better; neither, if we eat not, are we the worse.*

The New Testament does not teach us to follow the restrictions of the Law while accepting the grace of God given in Jesus Christ. Too many are still mixing Law and grace, which are totally opposites. The Law is condemnation and death, while grace is liberty and eternal life by faith in Jesus Christ. You cannot follow the Law and Christ! The Law brings death and points to Jesus Christ who brings life.

Romans 7:4: *Wherefore, my brethren, ye also are become dead to the law by the body of Christ; that ye should be married to another, even to him who is raised from the dead, that we should bring forth fruit unto God.*

We are told that all the dietary restrictions that were imposed by the Law were only temporary until Christ came and lifted the bondage of ordinances. Now, we are assured that the kingdom of God is not about meat or drink, but righteousness and peace in the Holy Ghost through Jesus Christ our Lord. Amen. In other words, God is not so much concerned about the foods you eat. What God is more interested in is faith in Christ: that you will repent and believe in His Son, Jesus Christ.

It is now up to the individual to eat whatever he wants. If his conscience tells him it's wrong to eat a certain food, then it is sin if he goes against the conviction of his conscience and eats it. But others who know the truth will not be convicted the same way as someone with a weak conscience.

Romans 14:1–3: *Him that is weak in the faith receive ye, but not to doubtful disputations. For one believeth that he may eat all things: another, who is weak, eateth herbs. Let not him that eateth despise him that eateth not; and let not him which eateth not judge him that eateth: for God hath received him.*

Romans 14:14: *I know, and am persuaded by the Lord Jesus, that there is nothing unclean of itself: but to him that esteemeth any thing to be unclean, to him it is unclean.*

For this cause, the Bible tells us to continue in the truth of the Word of God so that we might know the truth and be set free, because many will still confuse the Old Testament dietary restrictions with the liberty that has been given in Christ. Some will still teach others to abstain from certain foods because of lack of knowledge and doctrines of devils.

This cannot be more clearly stated than in the following passages:

1 Timothy: 4:1–6: *Now the Spirit speaketh expressly, that in the latter times some shall depart from the faith, giving heed to seducing spirits, and doctrines of devils; Speaking lies in hypocrisy; having their conscience seared with a hot iron; Forbidding to marry, and commanding to abstain from meats, which God hath created to be received with thanksgiving of them which believe and know the truth. For every creature of God is good, and nothing to be refused, if it be received with thanksgiving: For it is sanctified by the word of God and prayer. If thou put the brethren in remembrance of these things, thou shalt be a good minister of Jesus Christ, nourished up in the words of faith and of good doctrine, whereunto thou hast attained.*

1 Corinthians 10:27: *If any of them that believe not bid you to a feast, and ye be disposed to go; whatsoever is set before you, eat, asking no question for conscience sake.*

Christ is our Sabbath rest.

Another part of the gospel that creates confusion is regarding the Sabbath day or the day of rest. The Sabbath was also a shadow of greater things to come in Christ. It pointed to the new and everlasting covenant, established by the blood of Christ. It was made for man and not the other way around. Man was not made for the Sabbath. It wasn't meant to be a burden, as religion has made it out to be.

Jesus rebuked the religious leaders of His day for this. For example, the Seventh Day Adventists and Church of God have also adopted this doctrine of the Pharisees. If a Christian goes to church on Sunday instead of Saturday, does this mean that they have disobeyed the Ten Commandments and is therefore disqualified from entry into heaven, as some believe?

This is what some churches are teaching, which is not included in the gospel. Are we following the Law or living by the Spirit? This, again, is another problem that wants to frustrate the grace of God in Christ. As the Apostle Paul said, if righteousness came by the Law then Christ died in vain (**Galatians 2:21**).

The Bible tells us that some regard a certain day above others while others regard all days alike, but let every man be persuaded in his own mind. What this is saying is that it is not right or wrong to regard a certain day. This means you can worship on Sunday or Saturday if you want. Some prefer to gather on Sunday as the day of the resurrection of Christ, others still stick to the Old Testament Saturday, but this should not even be a major issue.

The Sabbath day is really a picture of the final day of rest in heaven. In heaven, there will not be any more night. It will be like one continuous day of rest. Moreover, our true rest is in Christ.

Romans 14:5: *One man esteemeth one day above another: another esteemeth every day alike. Let every man be fully persuaded in his own mind.*

Christ fulfilled the Sabbath day rest, which meant a certain day, was set apart and sanctified by God as holy. Under the Law, the day of rest had to be strictly obeyed or else death by stoning was the punishment.

Numbers 15:32–35: *And while the children of Israel were in the wilderness, they found a man that gathered sticks upon the sabbath day.*

And they that found him gathering sticks brought him unto Moses and Aaron, and unto all the congregation. And they put him in ward, because it was not declared what should be done to him. And the LORD said unto Moses, The man shall be surely put to death: all the congregation shall stone him with stones without the camp.

Jeremiah 17:21–22: *Thus saith the LORD; Take heed to yourselves, and bear no burden on the sabbath day, nor bring it in by the gates of Jerusalem; Neither carry forth a burden out of your houses on the sabbath day, neither do ye any work, but* *hallow ye the sabbath day, as I commanded your fathers.*

According to these Scriptures, no burden is to be borne on the Sabbath day because it is a day of rest; no work is to be done. When Jesus told the sick man in the gospel of John to take up his bed and walk, the religious leaders prosecuted Him for it, because healing was considered work. They charged Jesus for breaking the Sabbath, because He was working (doing miracles).

John 5:9-10: *And immediately the man was made whole, and took up his bed, and walked: and on the same day was the sabbath.*

The Jews therefore said unto him that was cured, It is the sabbath day: it is not lawful for thee to carry thy bed.

Why did Jesus work on the Sabbath day and then say that His Father also works? Doesn't the Old Testament say that God rested on the Sabbath day from all His work and we should do the same? Is there a contradiction here?

Jesus broke the Sabbath day by working, as it appears, contrary to the Law. Didn't Jesus say all the Law must be fulfilled? Doesn't the Old Testament say that no burden is to be carried into the gates of Jerusalem on the Sabbath day? Why did Jesus then tell the sick man to take up his bed on the Sabbath day?

Listen carefully! Listen to the Spirit! The Sabbath day was a sanctified day, set apart for the sanctification of sinners. This was the day of rest which God set apart for the redemption of sinners. The day that God, in the person of Jesus Christ, would rest in the grave for our sins to give us true rest from the burden of sin.

Psalm 38:4: *For mine iniquities are gone over mine head: as an heavy burden they are too heavy for me.*

The reason Jesus was working on the Sabbath was because God was working salvation in the midst of the earth, as was prophesied:

Psalm 74:12: *For God is my King of old, working salvation in the midst of the earth.*

Jesus worked on the Sabbath day because that was the day, set apart by God as holy, when God Himself would work salvation on earth.

The Pharisees did not understand the meaning of Sabbath and ran into the stumbling stone, as was also prophesied. There is no difference today. Many still stumble at the stumbling stone, Jesus Christ. They stumble at the Law and Christ. They still try to mix the two together.

Even though the Law says that no work is to be done on the Sabbath, Jesus proves to the Pharisees that none of them can keep the Sabbath, because if their sheep needed water or their ox had fallen into a pit on the Sabbath day, they themselves would break the Sabbath by rescuing them. Would they watch their animals die just because it's the Sabbath day and they are not allowed to even lift a straw on that day? I don't think so.

Luke 14:3–5: *And Jesus answering spake unto the lawyers and Pharisees, saying, Is it lawful to heal on the sabbath day? And they held their peace. And he took him, and healed him, and let him go; And answered them, saying, Which of you shall have an ass or an ox fallen into a pit, and will not straightway pull him out on the sabbath day?*

Luke 13:15: *The Lord then answered him, and said, Thou hypocrite, doth not each one of you on the sabbath loose his ox or his ass from the stall, and lead him away to watering?*

Matthew 12:11: *And he said unto them, What man shall there be among you, that shall have one sheep, and if it fall into a pit on the sabbath day, will he not lay hold on it, and lift it out?*

In the gospels, we see that Jesus made it clear to the Pharisees that their idea of keeping the Sabbath was not even logical, neither was it so ordained by God. It was a man-made hypocritical system that the

Pharisees invented to make themselves appear righteous, when they were truly wicked in their hearts.

External ordinances make the religious seem righteous in the sight of men, but God looks at the heart. Does anyone have to be reminded of this? If you are wicked in your heart, doesn't your conscience bear witness? The Pharisees made the Sabbath day a burden to the people, while making themselves appear righteous outwardly. Jesus was not pleased, and pronounced numerous woes on them. He asked them the question, "How can you escape the damnation of hell, you generation of vipers?" **Matthew 23:33** Their response should be: "We cannot".

They even tried to stop Jesus from healing on the Sabbath day, because they concluded that healing was work. Jesus asked them the question in **Mark 3:4:** "Is it lawful to do good on the Sabbath days, or to do evil? to save life, or to kill? But they held their peace."

When Jesus healed on the Sabbath day, in the religious leaders' understanding of the Sabbath, he broke the Sabbath, and they sought to kill Him for it.

John 5:18: *Therefore the Jews sought the more to kill him, because he not only had broken the Sabbath, but said also that God was his Father, making himself equal with God.*

The Pharisees, as well as many today, still don't understand the meaning of Sabbath. They were more concerned about the actual physical work, but forgot about the main theme of the Sabbath day, which is to refrain from evil and seek God with all your heart.

Mark 2:27–28: *And he said unto them, The sabbath was made for man, and not man for the sabbath: Therefore the Son of man is Lord also of the sabbath.*

Why did Jesus work on the Sabbath and say that the Sabbath was made for man and not man for the Sabbath?

The reason why Jesus could tell the sick to take up their bed and walk on the Sabbath was because He is Lord of the Sabbath. According to the Law, no one is supposed to carry any burden on the Sabbath day. When Jesus told the man to take up his bed and walk, the Pharisees told the man that it was against the Law, and they sought to prosecute Jesus for it. Everything written in the Law of Moses pertaining to the Sabbath day rest referred to Christ who came to give us true rest for our souls. When Jesus came, true rest came because true righteousness came.

The Law of the Sabbath forbids anyone from carrying any load or doing any work on the Sabbath day. Work or yoke under the Law means more than physical labor. It refers to the bondage or heaviness that sin brings upon an individual. Righteousness frees one from the load of sin. Christ is our righteousness and we no longer have to work for righteousness. We have been saved by His work on the cross and justified freely by His grace.

According to the book of Isaiah, honoring the Sabbath means to abstain from doing evil. It means doing the will of God, not your will. We are told to speak the words of God and honor Him. A person can refrain from physical work on a certain day, but if his heart is not pure and clean, he is not keeping the Sabbath.

Isaiah 56:2: *Blessed is the man that doeth this, and the son of man that layeth hold on it; that keepeth the sabbath from polluting it, and keepeth his hand from doing any evil.*

Isaiah 58:13–14: *If thou turn away thy foot from the sabbath, from doing thy pleasure on my holy day; and call the sabbath a delight, the holy of the LORD, honourable; and shalt honour him, not doing thine own ways, nor finding thine own pleasure, nor speaking thine own words: Then shalt thou delight thyself in the LORD; and I will cause thee to ride upon the high places of the earth, and feed thee with the heritage of Jacob thy father: for the mouth of the LORD hath spoken it.*

As a matter of fact, God told the children of Israel that the Sabbath was a sign between Him and them that God is the one who would sanctify them.

Exodus 31:13*: Speak thou also unto the children of Israel, saying, Verily my* ***sabbaths*** *ye shall keep: for it is* ***a sign*** *between me and you throughout your generations; that ye may know that I am the LORD that doth sanctify you.*

Ezekiel 20:12: *Moreover also I gave them my* ***sabbaths, to be a sign*** *between me and them, that they might know that I am the LORD that sanctify them.*

The Sabbath was a shadow and sign of something greater to come. It was a shadow of the true rest to be given in Christ. As Jesus said in **Matthew 11:28:** "Come unto me, all ye that labour and are heavy laden, and I will give you rest".

Hebrews 4:3: *For we which have believed do enter into rest, as he said, As I have sworn in my wrath, if they shall enter into my rest: although the works were finished from the foundation of the world.*

The Old Testament speaks of different signs; these signs pointed to Christ. Just as animals "without blemish" were a sign to the Lamb of God without blemish, so the Sabbath was a sign of rest for all who believe in Jesus.

For example, Jesus told the religious leaders that Jonah was in the fish's belly for three and three nights as a sign to His death, burial, and resurrection for three days.

Matthew 12:39-40: *But he answered and said unto them, An evil and adulterous generation seeketh after a sign; and there shall no sign be given to it, but the* ***sign*** *of the prophet Jonas: For as Jonas was three days and three nights in the whale's belly; so shall the Son of man be three days and three nights in the heart of the earth.*

Also, God says in the book of the Prophet Isaiah, that He would give a **sign** by which a virgin will bear a son called Immanuel. We know that this child was Jesus:

Isaiah 7:14: *Therefore the Lord himself shall give you a* ***sign****; Behold, a virgin shall conceive, and bear a son, and shall call his name Immanuel.*

Luke: 2:34: *And Simeon blessed them, and said unto Mary his mother, Behold, this child is set for the fall and rising again of many in Israel; and for a* ***sign*** *which shall be spoken against.*

God said in **Ezekiel 20:12** that the Sabbath was a sign between Him and the children of Israel that He is the one who sanctifies them. So then, we are not sanctified by our own works, but by the blood of Christ. Jesus confirmed this in His priestly prayer before His crucifixion. He fulfilled what was promised in Scriptures, that God would be the One to sanctify the people.

John 17:19: *And for their sakes I sanctify myself, that they also might be sanctified through the truth.*

Jesus prayed the Priestly prayer before His crucifixion, that we would be sanctified through Him. This was the promise God made to the children of Israel. He told them that the Sabbath was a sign to them that they might know that God is the One who sanctifies them. This sign of sanctification was pointing to the cross of Jesus Christ as being the way in which God Himself would sanctify His people (**Ezekiel 20:12, Exodus 31:13, Leviticus 20:8**).

Also, to further demonstrate this fact, in the book of Hebrews, we are told that the body of Christ, the body that was offered up for our sins, sanctifies us.

Hebrews 13:12: *Wherefore Jesus also, that he might sanctify the people with his own blood, suffered without the gate.*

When Jesus came, the Sabbath rest had finally come. We can now truly rest in God and speak God's words because of the gift of the Holy Spirit. By repenting of our sins and believing in Christ by faith, we can now rest in God. For this reason, Jesus invites everyone with the heavy burden of sin to take his yoke and find rest for their souls.

Matthew 11:28–29: *Come unto me, all ye that labour and are heavy laden, and*

I will give you rest. Take my yoke upon you, and learn of me; for I am meek and lowly in heart: and ye shall find rest unto your souls.

Honoring a day does not give one rest, but true rest comes by real faith in Christ. Why?

Faith in Christ eliminates the heavy burden that sin brings. If someone truly believes that God will forgive sins and provide all their needs, will he worry about food and raiment and judgment? Believing in Christ eliminates worries and burdens, and therefore rest for the soul is the outcome.

This rest is a gift from God that comes through the Holy Spirit. This happens when a person becomes a son or daughter of God through regeneration of the Holy Spirit, which comes only from God through Jesus Christ, the Prince of Peace (**Isaiah 9:6**). No man can offer this peace.

When a person becomes born again by the Holy Spirit, one of the fruits of the Spirit is the peace of God that surpasses all understanding. That peace results in rest for one's soul. This kind of peace does not depend on circumstances; it is a supernatural peace that is above human understanding.

Hebrews 4:3: *For we which have believed do enter into rest, as he said, As I have sworn in my wrath, if they shall enter into my rest: although the works were finished from the foundation of the world.*

Hebrews 4:10: *For he that is entered into his rest, he also hath ceased from his own works, as God did from his.*

The book of Hebrews tells us that if we cease from our own works and rest in Christ, which is righteousness and peace, we will enter that rest. So the whole point of resting, as commanded in the Law, by the keeping of the Sabbath as a carnal commandment, was to point us to the rest that would be given in Christ: spiritual rest.

CHAPTER 8

THE HOLY SPRIT AND THE LAW:

THE SPIRIT FULFILS THE LAW, SO WALK IN THE SPIRIT

Another part of the gospel that people become confused about pertains to the commandments that we are supposed to keep. Many are still teaching that we should try to keep the Ten Commandments, which is contrary to the Law of the Spirit of Christ.

Are we to follow the Law of Moses or follow the commands of Jesus in the New Testament?

The New Testament has much to say about this topic. The Apostle Paul said in ***Romans 8:3–4***, *that "what the law could not do, in that it was weak through the flesh, God sending His own Son in the likeness of sinful flesh, and for sin, condemned sin in the flesh: That the righteousness of the law might be fulfilled in us, who walk not after the flesh, but after the Spirit".*

He said that we are delivered from the Law that we might serve in newness of spirit. This means that we should walk in the Spirit. We are no longer under bondage to the Law, because we can't keep it anyway. The indwelling Spirit is what we live by. We now focus on being filled and led by the Spirit.

Romans 7:6: *But now we are delivered from the Law, that being dead wherein we were held; that we should serve in newness of spirit, and not in the oldness of the letter.*

But you ask, are you teaching me to break the Ten Commandments? No, I am telling you the Spirit of God causes us to obey God's commands, because we can't do it in the flesh. It is the Spirit who fulfils the Law in us. Listen to the promise God made regarding the new covenant of the Holy Spirit.

Hebrews 8:8–11: *For finding fault with them, he saith, Behold, the days come, saith the Lord, when I will make a new covenant with the house of Israel and with the house of Judah: Not according to the covenant that I made with their fathers in the day when I took them by the hand to lead them out of the land of Egypt; because they continued not in my covenant, and I regarded them not, saith the Lord. For this is the covenant that I will make with the house of Israel after those days, saith the Lord; I will put my laws into their mind, and write them in their hearts: and I will be to them a God, and they shall be to me a people: And they shall not teach every man his neighbour, and every man his brother, saying, Know the Lord: for all shall know me, from the least to the greatest.*

It is therefore quite clear in the new covenant that the keeping of the Law of God is done by the Spirit of God. God said that He would write them in our minds and hearts and cause us to obey Him. Don't complicate the simplicity of the gospel; our duty is to be led by the Spirit. If the Spirit leads us, we are not under the Law.

What would you do with the Holy Spirit of God, if you must keep the Law by your own sinful flesh? Obviously, you would have no use for the Holy Spirit, and have no power to live for God. You would become just like people of other religions.

Galatians 5:18: *But if ye be led of the Spirit, ye are not under the law.*

You might say, "Hold on a minute, didn't Jesus say to keep the commandments?"

Yes, Jesus commanded us to keep the commandments. The real question is, which ones? Many people will confuse the Law of Moses with the commands in the New Testament. Don't forget that we are not focused on trying to keep the Law and Ten Commandments; we are obeying what Jesus commanded us to do.

He didn't tell us to keep the Ten Commandments; He told us to walk in love. He made it clear that the whole Law is based on just two commands: love God and love your neighbor as yourself.

A young rich ruler came to Jesus and asked Him how to receive eternal life. Jesus told him to keep the commandments. The young man said he had kept them since he was a youth, but was still convicted that what he was doing was not good enough. Jesus told him that if he wanted to be perfect, he was to sell everything he had and follow Him.

Matthew 19:16–21: *And, behold, one came and said unto him, Good Master, what good thing shall I do, that I may have eternal life? And he said unto him, Why callest thou me good? there is none good but one, that is, God: but if thou wilt enter into life, keep the commandments. He saith unto him, Which? Jesus said, Thou shalt do no murder, Thou shalt not commit adultery, Thou shalt not steal, Thou shalt not bear false witness, Honour thy father and thy mother: and, Thou shalt love thy neighbour as thyself. The young man saith unto him, All these things have I kept from my youth up: what lack I yet? Jesus said unto him,* **If thou wilt be perfect,** *go and sell that thou hast, and give to the poor, and thou shalt have treasure in heaven: and come and follow me.*

What was missing in the young man's life was perfection. He wasn't perfect and his conscience bore witness that he broke the Law. Only the blood of Christ can make one perfect, as required by the Law.

What the young man needed to do was to get rid of his Law-keeping religion, get rid of his own way of thinking with regards to money and this worldly view of life, and follow Jesus who gives new life.

Deuteronomy 18:13: *Thou shalt be* **perfect** *with the LORD thy God.*

A lawyer also asked Jesus about the greatest commandment in the Law and Jesus said, "Love God and love your neighbor as yourself". Every time when Jesus was questioned about the Law, he always referred to love as the greatest commandment. As a matter of fact, He said all the Scriptures of the Law and Prophets hang on those two commandments.

Matthew 22:37–40: *Jesus said unto him, Thou shalt love the Lord thy God with all thy heart, and with all thy soul, and with all thy mind. This is the first and great commandment. And the second is like unto it, Thou shalt love thy neighbour as* *thyself. On these two commandments hang all the law and the prophets.*

Matthew 7:12: *Therefore all things whatsoever ye would that men should do to you, do ye even so to them: for this is the law and the prophets.*

What Jesus is saying is that the Ten Commandments are based on two commands: love God and love your neighbor as yourself. If you do both, you have fulfilled the Law.

The Apostle Paul further expanded on this topic, and states in many of his epistles, that love is the fulfillment of the Law.

Galatians 5:14: *For all the Law is fulfilled in one word, even in this; Thou shalt love thy neighbour as thyself.*

Romans 13:8–9: *Owe no man any thing, but to love one another: for he that loveth another hath fulfilled the Law. For this, Thou shalt not commit adultery, Thou shalt not kill, Thou shalt not steal, Thou shalt not bear false witness, Thou shalt not covet; and if there be any other commandment, it is briefly comprehended in this saying, namely, Thou shalt love thy neighbour as thyself.*

Whatever commandments Jesus tells us to keep in the New Testament, those are the commands we should obey. All the commands we are to keep are based on love. The Ten Commandments are based on love. **1 Corinthians 13** is the great love chapter that tells us that we can prophesy, do miracles, and other wonderful things in the spirit, but if we don't walk in love, we have done all these things in vain. You can honor a certain day as a Sabbath day, but if you don't walk in love, all is vain.

CHAPTER 9

ETERNAL JUDGMENT FOR REJECTING CHRIST

Although the gospel message declares the love of God through the death, burial, and resurrection of Christ to those who accept and believe, serious judgment awaits those who disbelieve. Jesus Himself preached a lot about eternal judgment in the furnace of fire, which many preachers are not preaching these days.

The whole point of Jesus dying on the cross and raised to majesty at the right hand of the Father in heaven is to deliver us from the eternal furnace of fire, which was already our default destination pronounced by the curse of the Law of Moses. Not preaching about everlasting fire gives people the impression that their default eternal destiny is not necessarily the lake of fire, and that they can enter heaven without going through Jesus Christ.

Jesus repeatedly warned us about eternal judgment:

Matthew 13:42: *And shall cast them into a furnace of fire: there shall be wailing and gnashing of teeth.*

Matthew 13:50: *And shall cast them into the furnace of fire: there shall be wailing and gnashing of teeth.*

Matthew 18:8–9: *Wherefore if thy hand or thy foot offend thee, cut them off, and cast them from thee: it is better for thee to enter into life halt or maimed, rather than having two hands or two feet to be cast into everlasting fire. And if thine eye offend thee, pluck it out, and cast it from thee: it is better for thee to enter into life with one eye, rather than having two eyes to be cast into hell fire.*

Matthew 25:41: *Then shall he say also unto them on the left hand, Depart from me, ye cursed, into* ***everlasting fire****, prepared for the devil and his angels.*

Revelation 14:11: *And the smoke of their torment ascendeth up for ever and ever: and they have no rest day nor night, who worship the beast and his image, and* *whosoever receiveth the mark of his name.*

Revelation 20:15: *And whosoever was not found written in the book of life was cast into the lake of fire.*

Revelation 21:8: *But the fearful, and unbelieving, and the abominable, and murderers, and whoremongers, and sorcerers, and idolaters, and all liars, shall have their part in the lake which burneth with fire and brimstone: which is the second death.*

It is quite evident from so many Scriptures in the gospels spoken by Jesus Himself, that eternal fire awaits those who don't repent and believe in Him. Many preachers would want to say Jesus loves everyone and will not cast them into the lake of fire, but that's not what Jesus said. It is very clear that God will seriously punish those who continue in sin, and will be greatly glorified and magnified in doing so, because HE is a God of judgment and justice.

God did not send His Son into the world for us to ignore Him and continue sinning without any future vengeance and retribution. Oh no, don't be deceived; God is very furious and angry against those who reject Jesus Christ and will eternally punish them for their sins.

Why do you think Jesus suffered so terribly on the cross? What do you think will happen to those who don't follow, obey, and love Jesus? Do you think they will also all go to heaven together with those who believe? Or do you think God will just annihilate them and they will cease to exist? It's way more serious that you might think; it's eternal punishment.

2 Thessalonians 1:7–9: *And to you who are troubled rest with us, when the Lord Jesus shall be revealed from heaven with his mighty angels,*

In flaming fire taking vengeance on them that know not God, and that obey not the gospel of our Lord Jesus Christ: Who shall be punished with **everlasting destruction** *from the presence of the Lord, and from the glory of his power.*

God is a God of Judgment and justice because He is holy.

As constantly repeated in Scriptures, God is holy and against sin. He totally hates it and will severely punish sinners. He makes it clear that evildoers will be punished for their evil, and that He will be known by the judgment which He executes (**Psalm 9:16**).

In God's kingdom, sin cannot exist; He must get rid of it so that His holiness will be magnified forever. As stated in ***Proverbs 20:8:*** *A king that sitteth in the throne of judgment scattereth away all evil with his eyes.* Well, God is that King who sits in the throne of Judgment to scatter all evil with His eyes.

Isaiah 61:8: *For I the LORD love judgment, I hate robbery for burnt offering; and I will direct their work in truth, and I will make an everlasting covenant with them.*

Psalm 37:28: *For the LORD loveth judgment, and forsaketh not his saints; they are preserved for ever: but the seed of the wicked shall be cut off.*

Psalm 9:7: *But the LORD shall endure forever: he hath prepared his throne for judgment.*

Psalm 9:16: *The LORD is known by the judgment which he executeth: the wicked is snared in the work of his own hands. Higgaion. Selah.*

Psalm 89:14: *Justice and judgment are the habitation of thy throne: mercy and truth shall go before thy face.*

Psalm 97:2: *Clouds and darkness are round about him: righteousness and judgment are the habitation of his throne.*

Proverbs 21:3: *To do justice and judgment is more acceptable to the LORD than sacrifice.*

God is angry and furious against those who don't put all their mind, body, and soul in worshipping Him and making Him the center of their lives. He is very wrathful against those who delight in sin and don't repent and come to His Son Jesus Christ to be cleansed.

Psalm 2:12: *Kiss the Son, lest he be angry, and ye perish from the way, when his wrath is kindled but a little. Blessed are all they that put their trust in him.*

1 Kings 11:9: *And the LORD was angry with Solomon, because his heart was turned from the LORD God of Israel, which had appeared unto him twice.*

2 Kings 17:18: *Therefore the LORD was very angry with Israel, and removed them out of his sight: there was none left but the tribe of Judah only.*

Psalm 7:11: *God judgeth the righteous, and God is angry with the wicked every day.*

Psalm 76:7: *Thou, even thou, art to be feared: and who may stand in thy sight when once thou art angry?*

Nahum 1:2: *God is jealous, and the LORD revengeth; the LORD revengeth, and is furious; the LORD will take vengeance on his adversaries, and he reserveth wrath for his enemies.*

Ezekiel 25:17: *And I will execute great vengeance upon them with furious rebukes; and they shall know that I am the LORD, when I shall lay my vengeance upon them.*

Micah 5:15: *And I will execute vengeance in anger and fury upon the heathen, such as they have not heard.*

Most preachers don't preach the entire gospel message of the love, mercy, and judgment of God. They don't want to warn the people about the seriousness of God's eternal judgment on those who refuse to come to Christ and be saved. Instead of preaching the entire gospel, all they talk about is the love of God. What about judgment for rejecting Christ?

The whole point of Jesus dying for our sins was for us to escape the eternal judgment of God in the lake of fire. As declared by the Law, we are all under condemnation and awaiting eternal judgment for our sins. For those who accept Christ, they have now been delivered from eternal judgment, while those who reject Him are awaiting everlasting punishment after death.

For this reason, warning people about their eternal punishment for not believing in Christ should be a main part of the gospel message. It should be the motivating factor for preaching the full message of the cross of Christ. That's what compelled the Apostle Paul so much, and all other great preachers.

As the Bible declares, today is the day of salvation. That's because none of us knows when we will die, that is to die without Christ and end up in hell fire.

Mark 6:11: *And whosoever shall not receive you, nor hear you, when ye depart thence, shake off the dust under your feet for a testimony against them. Verily I say unto you, It shall be more tolerable for Sodom and Gomorrha in the day of judgment, than for that city.*

1 Peter 4:17: *For the time is come that judgment must begin at the house of God: and if it first begin at us, what shall the end be of them that obey not the gospel of God?*

Jude 1:15: *To execute judgment upon all, and to convince all that are ungodly among them of all their ungodly deeds which they have ungodly committed, and of all their hard speeches which ungodly sinners have spoken against him.*

Hebrews 10:27: *But a certain fearful looking for of judgment and fiery indignation, which shall devour the adversaries.*

The Lord God executes fearful and terrible judgment against sin because of His uncompromising holiness.

All who believe in Christ must flee from sin. Although we have been forgiven of our sins by grace through faith in the blood of Christ, this does not mean that we have any excuse to continue in it. No child of God should continue in sin, because he/she is a representative of the righteousness of God.

Romans 6:1–2: *What shall we say then? Shall we continue in sin, that grace may abound? God forbid. How shall we, that are dead to sin, live any longer therein?*

Romans 6:6: *Knowing this, that our old man is crucified with him, that the body of sin might be destroyed, that henceforth we should not serve sin.*

Romans 6:13: *Neither yield ye your members as instruments of unrighteousness unto sin: but yield yourselves unto God, as those that are alive from the dead, and your members as instruments of righteousness unto God.*

2 Timothy 2:19: *Nevertheless the foundation of God standeth sure, having this seal, The Lord knoweth them that are his. And, Let every one that nameth the name of Christ depart from iniquity.*

Departing from iniquity is the main duty of Christians. If a person calls himself a Christian in name only, but is not concerned about his sins, then Jesus will say to that person on the day of Judgment: "Depart from me you who work iniquity, I don't know you". Sin is the main point. God sent His Son to deliver us from sin so that we can no longer live in it. But we are hearing a gospel today without the mention of the very thing that nailed Jesus to the cross.

CHAPTER 10

SUFFERING IS PART OF THE GOSPEL

There are many preachers talking about the good things or miracles that Jesus will do for people if they will just come to Him, as if Jesus came to make one's life better. Jesus says you must lose your life to gain eternal life. He didn't promise to make your life better, He promised to give you a new life.

This new life He promised is a journey filled with pain. It is a narrow way that is very rough, with constant battles and obstacles in the way. You are literally a soldier who is supposed to take up your sword and fight constantly against the Devil, the world, and the flesh.

Jesus said that those who truly follow Him would be persecuted. He never said it was an easy road. As a matter of fact, He promised tribulations would await those who faithfully follow Him. This means that following Christ does not protect a Christian from problems, but invites them instead. As a matter of fact, Jesus called Saul (Paul) to show him what tribulations he must suffer to enter the kingdom of heaven (**Acts 9:16**).

Jesus never said that following Him would eliminate troubles from one's life. Instead, He said many tribulations would come because of truly following Him. In addition, the Bible says God will put us through tribulations and trials to refine our faith, as gold is refined in the fire (**1 Peter 1, James 1**).

Remember what happened to Job, Joseph, and the rest of the prophets mentioned in the Old Testament and in the book of Hebrews, chapter 11? They went through much tribulation, but we see it was all ordained by God to fulfill His purpose.

In brief, the Bible tells us that being a real Christian is a fight to the end. Jesus says he who endures to the end will be saved (**Matthew 10:22**).

The Apostle Paul told Timothy to fight the good fight of faith (**1 Timothy 6:12**). You are in a war. You don't get to sit, relax, and take it easy. We are also told in another epistle that we are wrestling against principalities and powers.

Ephesians 6:12: *For we wrestle not against flesh and blood, but against principalities, against powers, against the rulers of the darkness of this world, against spiritual wickedness in high places.*

Matthew 24:9: *Then shall they deliver you up to be afflicted, and shall kill you: and ye shall be hated of all nations for my name's sake.*

Mark 13:11: *But when they shall lead you, and deliver you up, take no thought beforehand what ye shall speak, neither do ye premeditate: but whatsoever shall be given you in that hour, that speak ye: for it is not ye that speak, but the Holy Ghost.*

Matthew 10:28: *And fear not them which kill the body, but are not able to kill the soul: but rather fear him which is able to destroy both soul and body in hell.*

Mark 13:13: *And ye shall be hated of all men for my name's sake: but he that shall endure unto the end, the same shall be saved.*

John 17:14: *I have given them thy word; and the world hath hated them, because they are not of the world, even as I am not of the world.*

Jesus and the apostles tell us that persecution and suffering is a part of the gospel message. In other words, if we follow Jesus and want to share in His glory, we will also suffer. The children of God need to know this important truth, which is not being declared as it should be.

From the preaching that is going on today, we get the impression that Jesus came to give us abundant life that is filled with material things, and without any troubles. We have therefore concluded that Jesus came to give us our best pain-free life now, and that is what is called "the abundant life."

The abundant life is peace and joy in the Holy Ghost, not material wealth and life without problems. It is rejoicing in God for our eternal salvation through our Lord and Savior, Jesus Christ. The abundant life is having the life of God by the indwelling power of the Holy Spirit.

Since the Holy Spirit abides in us forever and ever, producing the fruits of joy, peace, love, etc., abundant life is therefore not dependent on our circumstances in life. It is dependent on being filled with the Spirit and producing the fruits of the Spirit.

Besides, Jesus already told us that we would weep and lament while the world would rejoice. In the end however, our situation will reverse, as in the case of the rich man and Lazarus. But now, we are citizens of heaven living in the enemy's territory. For this reason, we will be persecuted by the Devil and the world, because we are enemies of this world system.

It is important for those who want to follow Christ to know that testing, trials, and tribulations will come to them because they are not of this world. If you are not living a holy life, then don't worry about tribulations. The Apostle Paul, by the Holy Spirit, said if we live godly, we would suffer persecution as children of God in this evil world.

2 Timothy 3:12: *Yea, and all that will live godly in Christ Jesus shall suffer persecution.*

Philippians 1:29: *For unto you it is given in the behalf of Christ, not only to believe on him, but also to suffer for his sake;*

Philippians 3:10: *That I may know him, and the power of his resurrection, and the fellowship of his sufferings, being made conformable unto his death;*

Acts 9:16: *For I will shew him how great things he must suffer for my name's sake.*

Acts 5:41: *And they departed from the presence of the council, rejoicing that they were counted worthy to suffer shame for his name.*

Romans 8:17: *And if children, then heirs; heirs of God, and joint-heirs with Christ; if so be that we suffer with him, that we may be also glorified together.*

1 Thessalonians 3:4: *For verily, when we were with you, we told you before that* *we should suffer tribulation; even as it came to pass, and ye know.*

From all these verses, we can see undoubtedly that suffering is part of the Christian life. We are children of God and the light of the world. The whole world lies in darkness and does not like the light. In other words, the world lies in wickedness, and we are children of righteousness. These are in opposition of each other. If we shine the light into darkness, what do you think the darkness will do if it truly hates the light, as Jesus said?

This world is against God and Christ, so they will persecute you if you are really of God. Your reward is not on earth, it's in heaven. Jesus said those who are persecuted for His name's sake are blessed and have a great reward in heaven.

Matthew 5:11: *Blessed are ye, when men shall revile you, and persecute you, and shall say all manner of evil against you falsely, for my sake.*

Matthew 5:12: *Rejoice, and be exceeding glad: for great is your reward in heaven: for so persecuted they the prophets which were before you.*

CHAPTER 11

PASTORS, PREACH THE ENTIRE WORD OF GOD, THE FULL COUNSEL OF GOD!

Preaching the entire gospel message could cost you your life, but God tells us not to fear men neither worry about the death of the body—just preach the gospel. There is judgment against pastors who dilute the gospel and shy away from offending anyone, by not warning them about the fearful and eternal judgment of God for rejecting Christ.

Matthew 10:28: *And fear not them which kill the body, but are not able to kill the soul: but rather fear him which is able to destroy both soul and body in hell.*

From the beginning, God warned all His prophets to obey and proclaim everything He has commanded; that we should not diminish nor add to His Word. He has repeatedly commanded the prophets to proclaim His Word faithfully.

Jeremiah 23:28: *The prophet that hath a dream, let him tell a dream; and he that hath my word, let him speak my word faithfully. What is the chaff to the wheat? saith the LORD.*

Deuteronomy 12:32: *What thing soever I command you, observe to do it: thou shalt not add thereto, nor diminish from it.*

Not preaching about eternal judgment does not do the unsaved any good. It's the worst thing a preacher or minister of the gospel can do. What's the point of preaching? What kind of gospel are we really preaching? If God said to speak everything He has said in His Word, that's what we must do! That's why the church is still left on earth.

Ezekiel 3:17–18: *Son of man, I have made thee a watchman unto the house of Israel: therefore hear the word at my mouth, and give them warning from me. When I say unto the wicked, Thou shalt surely die; and thou givest him not warning, nor speakest to warn the wicked from his wicked way, to save his life; the same wicked* *man shall die in his iniquity; but his blood will I require at thine hand.*

Jeremiah 10:21: *For the pastors are become brutish, and have not sought the* LORD*: therefore they shall not prosper, and all their flocks shall be scattered.*

Jeremiah 12:10: *Many pastors have destroyed my vineyard, they have trodden my portion under foot, they have made my pleasant portion a desolate wilderness.*

Jeremiah 22:22: *The wind shall eat up all thy pastors, and thy lovers shall go into captivity: surely then shalt thou be ashamed and confounded for all thy wickedness.*

Jeremiah 23:1–2: *Woe be unto the pastors that destroy and scatter the sheep of my pasture! saith the* LORD*. Therefore thus saith the* LORD *God of Israel against the pastors that feed my people; Ye have scattered my flock, and driven them away, and have not visited them: behold, I will visit upon you the evil of your doings, saith the* LORD*.*

Micah 3:11: *The heads thereof judge for reward, and the priests thereof teach for hire, and the prophets thereof divine for money: yet will they lean upon the* LORD*, and say, Is not the* LORD *among us? none evil can come upon us.*

Malachi 2:7–9: *For the priest's lips should keep knowledge, and they should seek the law at his mouth: for he is the messenger of the* LORD *of hosts. But ye are departed out of the way; ye have caused many to stumble at the law; ye have corrupted the covenant of Levi, saith the* LORD *of hosts. Therefore have I also made you contemptible and base before all the people, according as ye have not kept my ways, but have been* ***partial in the law.***

Malachi 2:1–2: *And now, O ye priests, this commandment is for you. If ye will not hear, and if ye will not lay it to heart, to give glory unto my name, saith the* LORD *of hosts, I will even send a curse upon you, and I will curse your blessings: yea, I have cursed them already, because ye do not lay it to heart.*

As you can see in these Scriptures taken from **Jeremiah**, **Malachi**, and **Micah**, God is rebuking and warning pastors and priests for not feeding His sheep and being partial in the Law: teaching only on certain topics while avoiding the unpleasant ones. He is warning them of judgment for not warning the wicked to repent. God says many of these pastors and so-called "prophets" are doing the ministry for money and will be severely judged.

We cannot choose what we want to preach; we must preach all of God's Word, whether pleasant or unpleasant. We have chosen certain topics to preach while leaving out the ones we don't like. We cannot do this; God has already warned us to warn the wicked to turn from their wicked ways and come to Christ or they will die in hell. Tell them about hell and eternal judgment, not just that Jesus loves you.

It is sin not to obey and proclaim God's Word faithfully because of the fear of men. This was the sin of king Saul and that's why the kingdom was taken from him and given to king David.

1 Samuel 15:24–26: *And Saul said unto Samuel, I have sinned: for I have transgressed the commandment of the LORD, and thy words: because I feared the people, and obeyed their voice. Now therefore, I pray thee, pardon my sin, and turn again with me, that I may worship the LORD.*

And Samuel said unto Saul, I will not return with thee: for thou hast rejected the word of the LORD, and the LORD hath rejected thee from being king over Israel.

The gospel is the Word of God to be preached, not men's wisdom and so-called educated or eloquent speech.

The gospel message should not be preached by the enticing words of men's eloquent speech or wisdom, but by the power of the Holy Spirit. In other words, don't try to explain the gospel message in a way that is acceptable to sinners to avoid offending them about their current sinful state. The whole point of the gospel is to make people become sorrowful about their sins so that they can repent and believe in Jesus Christ in order that they might be saved.

This was what the Apostle Paul said to the churches, that he glories in the offensiveness of the cross of Christ as the only means of salvation and that if he was persecuted for doing so, he was very pleased and joyful in that. He said that he would not waver and would continue to proclaim the offensiveness of the gospel of Christ, whether people liked it or not.

1 Thessalonians 2:4: *But as we were allowed of God to be put in trust with the gospel, even so we speak; not as pleasing men, but God, which trieth our hearts.*

1 Corinthians 2:4: *And my speech and my preaching was not with enticing words of man's wisdom, but in demonstration of the Spirit and of power.*

Colossians 2:8: *Beware lest any man spoil you through philosophy and vain deceit, after the tradition of men, after the rudiments of the world, and not after Christ.*

Galatians 1:10: *For do I now persuade men, or God? or do I seek to please men? for if I yet pleased men, I should not be the servant of Christ.*

For sinners to come to the knowledge of their sinfulness, and their need of the Savior, Jesus Christ, the gospel must be proclaimed in its full offensiveness. We are not called to comfort sinners about their sins, but rather to let them come crawling to the altar with tears, mourning and confessing their sins to Christ, and then forsaking everything to follow Him.

The gospel is everlasting.

The gospel message is not just a message for this lifetime, but is everlasting. This message is the biggest news in the universe and will never end. It is bigger than we realize, and that's why people need to know it and truly honor and give glory to Christ, the everlasting King!

The reason is that the wounds Jesus bore on the cross are everlasting and bears witness to the marvelous greatness of God's love for us. So much so that He is willing to bear the scars of the cross in His body forever to further demonstrate that love.

When we get to heaven, we will still be talking about the cross, because we will see the wounds in Jesus' body. God has done it this way so that all who get to heaven will forever praise the Lamb that was slain to redeem them.

And so, we see that the cross is eternal and Christ will be forever exalted, praised, and glorified. All will stand in wonder and awe of Him! Of His power, His majesty, His glory, His wisdom, His beauty, His amazing love, and glorious wonder and riches of His redeeming grace through His shed blood on the cross.

1 Peter 1:25: *But the word of the Lord endureth forever. And this is the word, which by the gospel is preached unto you.*

Revelation 14:6: *And I saw another angel fly in the midst of heaven, having the everlasting gospel to preach unto them that dwell on the earth, and to every nation, and kindred, and tongue, and people.*

John 20:27: *Then saith he to Thomas, Reach hither thy finger, and behold my hands; and reach hither thy hand, and thrust it into my side: and be not faithless, but believing.*

Zechariah 13:6: *And one shall say unto him, What are these wounds in thine hands? Then he shall answer, Those with which I was wounded in the house of my friends.*

The gospel is the great mystery of God.

The work of the cross was already prophesied in the Old Testament as a wonder, which would not be believed. Yes, it is a mind-blowing mystery how God became a man and went to the cross to pay for our sins. I still stand in awe of it. It is way beyond all imagination!

Isaiah 29:14: *Therefore, behold, I will proceed to do a marvellous work among this people, even a marvellous work and a wonder: for the wisdom of their wise men shall perish, and the understanding of their prudent men shall be hid.*

The marvel and wonder of the gospel is that God became flesh in the person of Christ to die on the cross to redeem a people for Himself; a people for his own glory and praise. As **Ephesians 1** states:

Ephesians 1:6–7: *To the praise of the glory of his grace, wherein he hath made us accepted in the beloved. In whom we have redemption through his blood, the forgiveness of sins, according to the riches of his grace.*

The gospel is a great mystery, which angels desire to understand. It is just inconceivable. Therefore, don't try to preach a message that can be fully understood by men by using enticing words of men's wisdom. The only message that should be preached is the death, burial, and resurrection of Christ, which no creature, in heaven or on earth, can ever fully understand. It cannot be explained by mere human wisdom. The Holy Spirit, sent down from heaven, explains it.

Although we like to fully understand and explain everything before we accept and believe it, it is not so with the cross. I don't think any of us can explain how God became a man and died on the cross for our sins. The cross proves to us that God does things that no one can understand, so that we might stand in awe and fear of Him. That's why the cross is such a stumbling block to those who are perishing in their sins. They just see it as foolishness. Even greater foolishness to them is the claim that the One who died on the cross is the Creator Himself.

1 Corinthians 2:2: *For I determined not to know any thing among you, save Jesus Christ, and him crucified.*

1 Corinthians 2:7: *But we speak the wisdom of God in a mystery, even the hidden wisdom, which God ordained before the world unto our glory.*

1 Corinthians 2:13: *Which things also we speak, not in the words which man's wisdom teacheth, but which the Holy Ghost teacheth; comparing spiritual things with spiritual.*

Ephesians 6:19–20: *And for me, that utterance may be given unto me, that I may open my mouth boldly, to make known the mystery of the gospel,*

For which I am an ambassador in bonds: that therein I may speak boldly, as I ought to speak.

1 Peter 1:12: *Unto whom it was revealed, that not unto themselves, but unto us they did minister the things, which are now reported unto you by them that have preached the gospel unto you with the Holy Ghost sent down from heaven; which things the angels desire to look into.*

The mystery of the cross is so great that the Holy Spirit was sent down from heaven to explain it. This means that it was hidden from angels and other principalities and powers in heavenly places. In other words, only God (Holy Spirit) can explain God the Son (Jesus Christ crucified and resurrected).

As is explained in **Ephesians 3:9–10**, only the church of Christ is given the wisdom of the cross.

Ephesians 3:9–10: *And to make all men see what is the fellowship of the mystery, which from the beginning of the world hath been hid in God, who created all things by Jesus Christ: To the intent that now unto the principalities and powers in heavenly places might be known by the church the manifold wisdom of God.*

If we could understand all the things God does or is about to do, would we fear Him? Wouldn't we be just like God?

The book of **1 Peter** chapter 1 tells us that angels desire to look into the mystery of the gospel. If angels desire to look into it, can mortal man understand it with his own human mind?

The church is given the wisdom to understand the mystery of the cross, but we don't seem to be in awe or wonder of it; we still don't seem to be greatly amazed at this profound mystery. Preachers don't seem to understand the seriousness of sin and why the Son of God was the only One who was qualified to die to redeem us. For this reason, many churchgoers are not truly saved, neither are they excited about worshipping the Lamb that was slain.

Many churchgoers are not saved because they have not been told about God's judgment against sins and the serious consequence that they will bear for not repenting and turning away from them. The only message they hear in the church today is how much God loves them. They never hear about sin and eternal judgment because preachers don't understand the holiness of God, and they take the cross for granted.

Jesus talks about judgment, mercy, and faith, as being the weightier matters of the Law:

Matthew 23:23: *Woe unto you, scribes and Pharisees, hypocrites! for ye pay tithe of mint and anise and cummin, and have omitted the weightier matters of the law, judgment, mercy, and faith: these ought ye to have done, and not to leave the other undone.*

True repentance in turning away from sins and trusting in Jesus is the only way to be saved. This act, on the part of the sinner, will turn away the wrath of God. Without it, eternal judgment remains. One must be converted and become like a child to demonstrate that salvation has taken place. There must be a change in one's life.

Repentance and conversion was what Jesus and the apostles preached:

Luke 13:3: *I tell you, Nay: but, except ye repent, ye shall all likewise perish.*

Matthew 4:17: *From that time Jesus began to preach, and to say, Repent: for the kingdom of heaven is at hand.*

Matthew 11:21: *Woe unto thee, Chorazin! woe unto thee, Bethsaida! for if the mighty works, which were done in you, had been done in Tyre and Sidon, they would have repented long ago in sackcloth and ashes.*

Acts 3:19: *Repent ye therefore, and be converted, that your sins may be blotted out, when the times of refreshing shall come from the presence of the Lord.*

Even though we have heard constantly that God is love, we don't hear much about the wrath of God against those who don't truly repent and turn their heart fully to Him. Not everyone is going to heaven. Many people are on their way to hell. This is because we have forgotten about sin and repentance. We seem to have forgotten that God is holy. God loves us so much that He sent His Son to die for our sins so that we might repent and walk in His holiness.

If we don't repent, we will end up in the lake of fire. The lake of fire does not display the love of God; it displays His full wrath. Let's start talking about the holiness of God and why the need for the cross. The judgment of God is very, very serious.

I'm sure none of us would like to see the wrath of God. Who can stand before Him when He stands to judge? Who can abide His indignation? That Day will be great and terrible; there will never be a day like that. Are you able to withstand His wrath? I sure can't, and I really don't want to experience it personally, neither do I want any human being to experience eternal destruction.

Repentance means feeling sorrowful for your sins so much that you immediately turn away from them. It means that you hate your sins so much that you become mournful about your condition and gladly embrace the cross.

2 Corinthians 7:10: *For godly sorrow worketh repentance to salvation not to be repented of: but the sorrow of the world worketh death.*

Not only should one accept the sacrifice of Jesus as the payment for their sins, it means handing over your life to Christ and dying to yourself. As a result, your will and personal desires are also dead. You now are to do everything for the sake of Christ, not yourself. It means denying yourself.

Colossians 3:3: *For ye are dead, and your life is hid with Christ in God.*

2 Timothy 2:11: *It is a faithful saying: For if we be dead with him, we shall also live with him:*

1 Corinthians 6:20: *For ye are bought with a price: therefore glorify God in your body, and in your spirit, which are God's.*

Romans 6:8: *Now if we be dead with Christ, we believe that we shall also live* *with him.*

Romans 12:2: *And be not conformed to this world: but be ye transformed by the renewing of your mind, that ye may prove what is that good, and acceptable, and perfect, will of God.*

Revelation 9:20: *And the rest of the men which were not killed by these plagues yet repented not of the works of their hands, that they should not worship devils, and idols of gold, and silver, and brass, and stone, and of wood: which neither can see, nor hear, nor walk:*

Revelation 2:16: *Repent; or else I will come unto thee quickly, and will fight against them with the sword of my mouth.*

The way the gospel is being preached today does not bring about true conviction of sins, but restricts the work of the Holy Spirit. If sin, judgment, and righteousness are not preached, true conviction of sins and the fear of God, brought about by the Holy Spirit, cannot take place. The Holy Spirit is the One who convicts the world of sin, righteousness, and judgment.

Therefore, the preacher's duty is to tell the sinners, from the Word of God, their terrible state of condemnation because of sin, and their need to be forgiven through the cross, the only way prescribed by God, to avert eternal judgment and enter eternal life and peace with God. When this truth is preached, the Holy Spirit begins to work.

John 16:7–8: *Nevertheless I tell you the truth; It is expedient for you that I go away: for if I go not away, the Comforter will not come unto you; but if I depart, I will send him unto you. And when he is come, he will reprove the world of sin, and of righteousness, and of judgment.*

Some preachers don't fully understand the cross, neither do they understand sound doctrine, and lack the power of the Holy Spirit as a result. Our God is a God of truth and justice. He already warned the prophets of old that whatever He has commanded them to speak, speak every word. Don't leave anything out.

Today's preachers don't want to offend sinners. For this reason, the Holy Spirit cannot work in the church, because the Holy Spirit is holy and is against sin. He is the one who convicts the world of sin, not the enticing words of men.

Because Christ has fulfilled the Old Testament, most churches only preach the New Testament. Consequently, they don't have sound doctrine and lack full understanding of the cross. The Old Testament is very important because we all need to know that all the ordinances in the sacrificial system outlined in the book of Leviticus speak of the cross. In addition, all the stories in the Old Testament are pictures of the cross. I mean, all those stories that we can't seem to make sense of testify of the sufferings of Christ.

We must understand the seriousness of sin as outlined in the Law. **Romans 3:20** tells us that by the Law is the knowledge of sin; therefore, we need to understand how sinful we are, how holy God is, and why such a holy, holy, holy God would lay down His life for us.

I must admit that the cross never ceases to amaze me when I think of its monumental display of God's love, which far exceeds human love and our ability to comprehend the love of God. It shows me that my praises are just not adequate to express how worthy God is of all glory, honor, praises, blessings, and dominion forever. I just stand truly amazed at the cross.

According to the Law of Moses, every sin requires the shedding of blood before forgiveness can be granted. This means telling a lie, no matter how small or how big one might think that is, requires the shedding of blood. This was done to reveal the seriousness of sin and the uncompromising holiness of God. As the Law states, the penalty of sin is death.

Leviticus 4:3: *If the priest that is anointed do sin according to the sin of the people; then let him bring for his sin, which he hath sinned, a young bullock without blemish unto the* LORD *for a sin offering.*

Leviticus 4:34: *And the priest shall take of the blood of the sin offering with his finger, and put it upon the horns of the altar of burnt offering, and shall pour out all the blood thereof at the bottom of the altar.*

Leviticus 5:5–6: *And it shall be, when he shall be guilty in one of these things, that he shall confess that he hath sinned in that thing: And he shall bring his trespass offering unto the* LORD *for his sin which he hath sinned, a female from the flock, a lamb or a kid of the goats, for a sin offering; and the priest shall make an atonement for him concerning his sin.*

Leviticus 4:22–23: *When a ruler hath sinned, and done somewhat through ignorance against any of the commandments of the* LORD *his God concerning things which should not be done, and is guilty; Or if his sin, wherein he hath sinned, come to his knowledge; he shall bring his offering, a kid of the goats, a male without blemish.*

Leviticus 4:27–28: *And if any one of the common people sin through ignorance, while he doeth somewhat against any of the commandments of the* LORD *concerning things which ought not to be done, and be guilty; Or if his sin, which he hath sinned, come to his knowledge: then he shall bring his offering, a kid of the goats, a female without blemish, for his sin which he hath sinned.*

Leviticus 26:27–28: *And if ye will not for all this hearken unto me, but walk contrary unto me; Then I will walk contrary unto you also in fury; and I, even I, will chastise you seven times for your sins.*

Deuteronomy 27:26: *Cursed be he that confirmeth not all the words of this Law to do them. And all the people shall say, Amen.*

As demonstrated in the Law of Moses, various sacrificial animals without blemish were continually offered up for sins. In addition to the numerous sacrifices required for every sin committed, many other ordinances were also to be observed. This was meant to give us an understanding of the severity of the punishment for sins, but was only a shadow of the true eternal death that will take place at the Great White Throne Judgment.

Breaking the Law means death, as shown in the Old Testament. Breaking the Law of God is sin, and sin is death. Under the curse of the Law, many died immediately for their sins because the Law came to issue judgment for sins.

Numbers 26:61: *And Nadab and Abihu died, when they offered strange fire before the LORD.*

Numbers 15:36: *And all the congregation brought him (Sabbath-breaker gathering sticks, v.* ***32****) without the camp, and stoned him with stones, and he died; as the LORD commanded Moses.*

Numbers 26:10: *And the earth opened her mouth, and swallowed them up together with Korah, when that company died, what time the fire devoured two hundred and fifty men: and they became a sign.*

Numbers 16:49: *Now they that died in the plague were fourteen thousand and seven hundred, beside them that died about the matter of Korah.*

Numbers 21:6: *And the LORD sent fiery serpents among the people, and they bit the people; and much people of Israel died.*

The main point of the Old Testament Scriptures, especially the sacrificial system in the Law of Moses, is to reveal to us that God is totally pure and holy. For every sin committed according to the Law, the sacrificial offering of blood was required as atonement. The Law shows us how sinful we are and how holy God is.

Curses were issued for not obeying any of the commandments, and all the people agreed by saying Amen. When these curses were sealed by the children of Israel declaring "Amen", all people were cursed as a result. Since we have all disobeyed the Law, we are eternally cursed: the most serious matter we must deal with. We all need to have this curse removed.

To demonstrate God's holiness, when even Moses sinned, he could not enter the promised land but died. Aaron's two sons also died when they offered the wrong incense to the Lord. Aaron also died when he trespassed against the Lord at the waters of Meribah-Kadesh (**Numbers 20:24–29**). Furthermore, most of the children of Israel died for disobeying the commandments as examples of the holiness of God and how He expects us to fully obey Him.

We are told that many of the Israelites died for complaining and murmuring against God. All these examples of the Old Testament are given to teach us to be holy and perfect as God is holy and perfect. Obviously, none of us can ever achieve total perfection because we are naturally sinful and like to choose our own way.

That's why Jesus fulfilled the Law on our behalf. He was the Lamb of God without blemish offered up for our sins, and the only One who perfectly obeyed and fulfilled all requirements of the Law to please God the Father. For this reason, the righteousness of Christ is imputed to anyone who repents and believes in Him.

CHAPTER 12

THE CROSS OF CHRIST HAS FULFILLED THE REQUIREMENTS OF THE LAW

The Bible tells us that we were enemies of God and deserved eternal punishment according to the Law, but Christ has made us children of God through His death, burial, and resurrection.

Colossians 1:21–23: *And you, that were sometime alienated and enemies in your mind by wicked works, yet now hath he reconciled In the body of his flesh through death, to present you holy and unblameable and unreproveable in his sight: If ye continue in the faith grounded and settled, and be not moved away from the hope of the gospel, which ye have heard, and which was preached to every creature which is under heaven; whereof I Paul am made a minister.*

Romans 5:10: *For if, when we were enemies, we were reconciled to God by the death of his Son, much more, being reconciled, we shall be saved by his life.*

Don't miss the fact that God had pronounced us His enemies by the Law because of the thoughts of our minds. In other words, our thinking was enough to convict us of eternal judgment. Don't get the idea that the Law was given to make us righteous and that God was well pleased with our good deeds. As a matter of fact, the Law was a curse to us. The Law is good, but we are evil. As God said by the mouth of Jeremiah, "Can you being evil, do good?"

Jeremiah 13:23: *Can the Ethiopian change his skin, or the leopard his spots? then may ye also do good, that are accustomed to do evil.*

Can you see what God is saying? He is asking the question: Can the Ethiopian change his skin or the leopard his spots? The answer is obviously: NO. They were born that way. God asked that question to bring up the next point about us. The real question is: Can we, who are accustomed to doing evil, do any good? The answer again is: NO! We were born that way. That's what makes the Law a curse to us.

Galatians 3:10–13: *For as many as are of the works of the law are under the curse: for it is written, Cursed is every one that continueth not in all things which are written in the book of the law to do them. But that no man is justified in the sight of God, it is evident: for, The just shall live by faith. And the law is not of faith: but, The man that doeth them shall live in them. Christ hath redeemed us from the curse of the law, being made a curse for us: for it is written, Cursed is every one that hangeth on a tree.*

All the tedious ordinances in the Law that were impossible for us to keep, Christ has also nailed to the cross and has made us free from the bondage of ordinances. We now live and walk in the Spirit, not by performing ordinances of the Law.

Ephesians 2:15: *Having abolished in his flesh the enmity, even the law of commandments contained in ordinances; for to make in himself of twain one new man, so making peace.*

Colossians 2:14: *Blotting out the handwriting of ordinances that was against us, which was contrary to us, and took it out of the way, nailing it to his cross.*

The ordinances were so tedious and lengthy, that the job of the priest was more than a full-time job. For example, **Leviticus 14** gives instructions to the priest on how to cleanse a leper from leprosy, and it is 32 verses long, and is only one of the many ordinances that must be strictly followed.

Christ also fulfilled the Sabbath.

The keeping of the Sabbath day has become such a big concern for many in Christendom, and has even caused division. Some will argue that the keeping of Saturday is very vital in the New Covenant as it was in the old, making it seem as if it is a very essential part in Jesus' commandments. So vital that if we worship on Sunday, we have taken the mark of the beast and are very well on the way to hell. Is it as vital as some say it is? Does our salvation depend on the observance of Saturday as a special day that truly must be kept?

In the Law of Moses, we were commanded to keep the Sabbath day, which was a sanctified day of rest. According to the New Testament, the Sabbath was only a shadow of the true spiritual rest that we now have by faith in Christ. We are told that true rest does not come from honoring a certain day, but trusting and believing in Christ by faith.

In the Old Testament, we were commanded to keep the Sabbaths as a sign between the children of Israel and God that God would be the one to sanctify them.

Before Jesus went to the cross, He prayed to the Father in **St. John 17**, that he would sanctify us. Also, in **Hebrews 13:12**, we are told that Jesus, the Lord, sanctified us by His own blood.

Therefore, Jesus, the Eternal God, fulfilled His promise regarding the Sabbath of the Old Testament.

God told the children of Israel that the Sabbath was a sign. A sign points in the direction of the real thing. It is not the real thing; it is only a pointer. In other words, the Sabbath, which was a sanctified day of rest, pointed to the day which God had sanctified and set apart as the day He would sanctify His people by His own blood.

This was the day that God would rest in the grave. That's why Jesus was in the grave on the Sabbath day. He rose on the first day. Therefore, we see the Sabbath fulfilled in Christ, as the following Scriptures show:

Exodus 31:13: *Speak thou also unto the children of Israel, saying, Verily my Sabbaths ye shall keep: for it is a sign between me and you throughout your generations; that ye may know that I am the LORD that doth sanctify you.*

John 17:19: *And for their sakes I sanctify myself, that they also might be sanctified through the truth.*

Hebrews 13:12: *Wherefore Jesus also, that he might sanctify the people with his own blood, suffered without the gate.*

There are many mysteries in the Bible that we don't understand because they have not yet been revealed to us. Just when you think you understand something, you find out that you have not even truly started. The Bible was written by the Holy Spirit and contains deep things of the Spirit of God. We are warned not to be babies, but to grow up in the Spirit. Even Paul warned the Corinthian church that he couldn't say much to them from the Scriptures because they were not ready to receive it, since they were not mature enough to understand (**1 Corinthians 3**).

The meaning of Sabbath day rest has confused many people. The honoring of a certain day as the Sabbath is an external, carnal commandment, but we are under a new covenant, a spiritual Law, which is internal, and of the heart. For this reason, the New Testament tells us not to judge anyone regarding eating certain meat, or honoring a certain day as the Sabbath day.

Colossians 2:16: *Let no man therefore judge you in meat, or in drink, or in respect of an holyday, or of the new moon, or of the sabbath days.*

Romans 14:5–6: *One man esteemeth one day above another: another esteemeth every day alike. Let every man be fully persuaded in his own mind. He that regardeth the day, regardeth it unto the Lord; and he that regardeth not the day, to the Lord he doth not regard it. He that eateth, eateth to the Lord, for he giveth God thanks; and he that eateth not, to the Lord he eateth not, and giveth God thanks.*

Acts 15:24: *Forasmuch as we have heard, that certain which went out from us have troubled you with words, subverting your souls, saying, Ye must be circumcised, and keep the law: to whom we gave no such commandment.*

The point given in **Romans 14:5–6** is one of preference regarding a certain day. If you choose Saturday as your day of rest to the Lord, then fine, but don't go around condemning those who regard Sunday. This also goes for those who honor Sunday. The real question is: are you born again of the Spirit of God and have been adopted into God's Family as one of His children?

Jesus gives life but the Law brings death.

There are many who still confuse Law and grace. The Bible says if you have received Jesus Christ as Lord and Savior, you are dead to the Law. You cannot follow the Law while living under grace.

This was the message the beloved Apostle Paul tried to get to the Galatian church.

Galatians 2:19: *For I through the law am dead to the law, that I might live unto God.*

The Law came in to reveal to us that sin is death. The Apostle Paul states that before the Law came in, he was alive, but after it came into effect, it killed him. In other words, the Law came to reveal the exceeding sinfulness of sin and to punish the sinners for breaking God's Law. How then can anyone follow the Law to receive eternal life?

Romans 7:9: *For I was alive without the law once: but when the commandment came, sin revived, and I died.*

Romans 8:3-4: *For what the law could not do, in that it was weak through the flesh, God sending his own Son in the likeness of sinful flesh, and for sin, condemned sin in the flesh: That the righteousness of the law might be fulfilled in us, who walk not after the flesh, but after the Spirit.*

When God became a man, and went to the cross to redeem us from sin, it became a great mystery to angels who desire to consider it.

Angels are amazed at the gospel because Jesus was God who took the form of man and died on the cross to pay for the sins of sinful men who were made lower than the angels. If God did not redeem the angels that rebelled against Him in heaven, surely He would not redeem men, would He?

1 Peter 1:12: *Unto whom it was revealed, that not unto themselves, but unto us they did minister the things, which are now reported unto you by them that have preached the gospel unto you with the Holy Ghost sent down from heaven; which* *things the angels desire to look into.*

The reason why the cross is such a mystery to the angels is because they know that God is holy, and executes swift judgment against all who rebel against Him. They are very aware of this because they are the ones who sing "Holy, holy, holy, Lord God Almighty", constantly forever before the throne.

Revelation 4:8: *And the four beasts had each of them six wings about him; and they were full of eyes within: and they rest not day and night, saying, Holy, holy, holy, Lord God Almighty, which was, and is, and is to come.*

Isaiah 6:2–3: *Above it stood the seraphims: each one had six wings; with twain he covered his face, and with twain he covered his feet, and with twain he did fly. And one cried unto another, and said, Holy, holy, holy, is the LORD of hosts: the whole earth is full of his glory.*

The elect angels also know that when the other angels, Lucifer and his host of angels sinned, they were immediately cast out of heaven and reserved for eternal destruction in the lake of fire. God did not spare them in order that He might show them mercy and redemption when they sinned, but immediately reserved them for eternal destruction.

2 Peter 2:4: *For if God spared not the angels that sinned, but cast them down to hell, and delivered them into chains of darkness, to be reserved unto judgment…*

Jude 1:6: *And the angels which kept not their first estate, but left their own habitation, he hath reserved in everlasting chains under darkness unto the judgment of the great day.*

The angels don't understand why such a holy God would take such pleasure in sinful man and ask the question:

Hebrews 2:6: *But one in a certain place testified, saying, What is man, that thou art mindful of him? or the son of man, that thou visitest him?*

Psalm 8:4–5: *What is man, that thou art mindful of him? and the son of man, that thou visitest him? For thou hast made him a little lower than the angels, and* *hast crowned him with glory and honour.*

Job 7:17: *What is man, that thou shouldest magnify him? and that thou shouldest set thine heart upon him?*

One reason why God has taken pleasure in sinful man is to demonstrate His love that surpasses our human knowledge, and to make His wisdom known to principalities and powers in heavenly place through the church, His purchased possession.

As you can see, the angels are perplexed as to why a holy, holy, holy Almighty God would set his heart upon sinful man to even be mindful of him when the other angels that sinned are awaiting eternal punishment, never to be redeemed.

Jesus, the Lamb of God, alone is worthy of all praise, which will be fully confirmed at His second coming.

We do not understand the scope of the cross, but it is the greatest event that ever took place in the universe. So great is the cross that the new song that is being sung in heaven is about the Lamb that was slain. In plain terms, all the singing and worshipping that's taking place in heaven is about the cross. It's all about the Lamb who was slain to redeem people from all nations, tribes, and tongues, from the four corners of the earth.

Revelation 5:8–14: *And when he had taken the book, the four beasts and four and twenty elders fell down before the Lamb, having every one of them harps, and golden vials full of odours, which are the prayers of saints. And they sung a new song, saying, Thou art worthy to take the book, and to open the seals thereof: for thou wast slain, and hast redeemed us to God by thy blood out of every kindred, and tongue, and people, and nation; And hast made us unto our God kings and priests: and we shall reign on the earth. And I beheld, and I heard the voice of many angels round about the throne and the beasts and the elders: and the number of them was ten thousand times ten thousand, and thousands of thousands; Saying with a loud voice, Worthy is the Lamb that was slain to receive power, and riches, and wisdom, and* *strength, and honour, and glory, and blessing. And every creature which is in heaven, and on the earth, and under the earth, and such as are in the sea, and all that are in them, heard I saying, Blessing, and honour, and glory, and power, be unto him that sitteth upon the throne, and unto the Lamb for ever and ever. And the four beasts said, Amen. And the four and twenty elders fell down and worshipped him that liveth for ever and ever.*

Revelation 7:9–12: *After this I beheld, and, lo, a great multitude, which no man could number, of all nations, and kindreds, and people, and tongues, stood before the throne, and before the Lamb, clothed with white robes, and palms in their hands; And cried with a loud voice, saying, Salvation to our God which sitteth upon the throne, and unto the Lamb. And all the angels stood round about the throne, and about the elders and the four beasts, and fell before the throne on their faces, and worshipped God, Saying, Amen: Blessing, and glory, and wisdom, and thanksgiving, and honour, and power, and might, be unto our God for ever and ever. Amen.*

If all creatures in heaven fall down and worship the Lamb, what about us on the earth? Yes, everyone should worship Him because of what He did on the cross for us sinners. That's not the only reason to worship Him, but it is the one overwhelming reason by which all the redeemed stand to praise.

Many people don't even like to hear the name of Jesus. They don't acknowledge Him as being worthy of worship. There are many anti-Christ religions all over the world that will not bow down and worship Jesus, but they will see one day that He is more than worthy, as declared in the following verses:

Philippians 2:8–11: *And being found in fashion as a man, he humbled himself, and became obedient unto death, even the death of the cross. Wherefore God also hath highly exalted him, and given him a name which is above every name: That at the name of Jesus every knee should bow, of things in heaven, and things in earth, and things under the earth; And that every tongue should confess that Jesus Christ is Lord, to the glory of God the Father.*

Anyone who refuses to worship and give glory to the Lamb will suffer eternal destruction. In other words, the cross demands that all living creatures in heaven, earth, and under the earth worship the Lord Jesus Christ with all their might! The Lamb will return to execute wrath Himself against those who refuse and disobey!

Revelation 6:15–16: *And the kings of the earth, and the great men, and the rich men, and the chief captains, and the mighty men, and every bondman, and every free man, hid themselves in the dens and in the rocks of the mountains; And said to the mountains and rocks, Fall on us, and hide us from the face of him that sitteth on the throne, and from the wrath of the Lamb.*

Revelation 16:9: *And men were scorched with great heat, and blasphemed the name of God, which hath power over these plagues: and they repented not to give him glory.*

There is no power in the church because we don't worship God the way we should because of not knowing about the greatness of the cross. God wants us to have full knowledge of His everlasting salvation so that we can fully praise Him as much as we are able.

We are to increase in the knowledge of His grace, because it is so amazing and of such eternal value that it is truly worth seeking after above all else; it is way beyond this life. There is so much that awaits the redeemed in eternity, but we need to know the riches of His grace in order that we might exceedingly praise and worship Him now.

Think strongly about this: If all the angels in heaven are singing a new song about the Lamb that was slain, falling on their faces before the throne and "Saying with a loud voice, Worthy is the Lamb that was slain to receive power, and riches, and wisdom, and strength, and honor, and glory, and blessing" (**Revelation 5:12**), how about us? Shouldn't we worship more since we are the ones who have been redeemed by the blood of the Lamb?

The cross is the power and wisdom of God demonstrated through His church by the Holy Spirit.

Loving, adoring, and worshipping the Lord Jesus Christ and testifying of the blood that He shed on the cross to redeem us from sin is the power of the gospel. Only when the cross is proclaimed does the power of the Holy Spirit flow.

The cross testifies of the holiness of God—His righteousness, judgment, love, and justice against sin. As a result, when the work of the cross is fully preached, the Holy Spirit begins to move and to convict sinners of sin.

It is not the preachers' duty to try and convince people to come to Christ by using their own flattering words. The Holy Spirit brings conviction to sinners by the way of the preaching of the cross. This was demonstrated in the book of Acts.

Acts 2:36–8: *Therefore let all the house of Israel know assuredly, that God hath made that same Jesus, whom ye have crucified, both Lord and Christ.*

Now when they heard this, they were pricked in their heart, and said unto Peter and to the rest of the apostles, Men and brethren, what shall we do? Then Peter said unto them, Repent, and be baptized every one of you in the name of Jesus Christ for the remission of sins, and ye shall receive the gift of the Holy Ghost.

Acts 10:43–44: *To him give all the prophets witness, that through his name whosoever believeth in him shall receive remission of sins.*

While Peter yet spake these words, the Holy Ghost fell on all them which heard the word.

When the Apostle Peter preached the cross on the day of Pentecost, the Holy Spirit moved and brought about the conviction of sin to the hearts of 3 thousand and 5 thousand souls, respectively. They repented and received the Lord Jesus as Savior and Lord of all.

We, the church of Christ, need to learn how to worship and give glory to the Lamb, as described in the book of Revelation. The only way we can learn to worship is if we gain more knowledge of the cross.

Revelation 19:5: *And a voice came out of the throne, saying, Praise our God, all ye his servants, and ye that fear him, both small and great.*

1Peter 2:9: *But ye are a chosen generation, a royal priesthood, an holy nation, a peculiar people; that ye should shew forth the praises of him who hath called you out of darkness into his marvellous light:*

Hebrews 13:15: *By him therefore let us offer the sacrifice of praise to God continually, that is, the fruit of our lips giving thanks to his name.*

We have become a church that conforms to the change in society by limiting our prayer and worship services to spend more time seeking material things. In addition, we are not spending enough time studying the Word of God, and as a result, we lack the understanding of the mercy that has been granted to us through the cross. We don't seem to understand that we were literally seriously dead, and Christ redeemed us from everlasting fire to everlasting life. We believe that we have a right to live!

God's eternal judgment awaits those who reject Jesus Christ.

The Holy Spirit is given to testify who Jesus is and what He has done for sinners, when He left the glory of the Father in heaven, and became one of us to redeem us to God by His own blood. Those who receive Him have eternal life and joy, but those who reject Him are eternally cursed. Everyone who rejects Christ has a great price to pay and cannot forfeit that payment.

The punishment for rejecting Christ is everlasting torment in a lake of fire. This means that truthful proclamation of the gospel is a very serious duty given to those who are called by God to declare the message of salvation in Christ. God's punishment is forever. It is very difficult to grasp and come to terms with, but that's the reality.

Matthew 25:41: *Then shall he say also unto them on the left hand, Depart from me, ye cursed, into everlasting fire, prepared for the devil and his angels.*

Matthew 25:46: *And these shall go away into everlasting punishment: but the righteous into life eternal.*

Revelation 20:10: *And the devil that deceived them was cast into the lake of fire and brimstone, where the beast and the false prophet are, and shall be tormented day and night for ever and ever.*

Revelation 14:10: *The same shall drink of the wine of the wrath of God, which is poured out without mixture into the cup of his indignation; and he shall be tormented with fire and brimstone in the presence of the holy angels, and in the presence of the Lamb.*

Revelation 20:15: *And whosoever was not found written in the book of life was cast into the lake of fire.*

The lake of fire is the final eternal destination of all who refuse to come to Christ and be saved. It is for the Devil and his angels and all Christ rejecters. It is a real place of eternal sufferings. Due to the severity of God's eternal punishment, faithful proclamation of the entire gospel is a very serious duty given to those called by God, especially those who stand on the altar to preach: evangelists, pastors, and teachers.

With such an eternal weight of judgment against sinners, many ministers still shy away from the doctrine of eternal judgment, even though one day we will all have to face God and give an account for how we handled the message of the gospel entrusted to us. The judgment of God is the most serious matter ever to contend with, and not to be taken lightly.

We cannot change the message. We must declare the full counsel of God: the things we don't want to hear and the things that our ears are itching to hear. I don't think anyone would want to hear that there is a lake of fire that burns forever awaiting those who don't repent and put their faith in Jesus Christ.

People don't want to hear that, but that reality is not from men, it's from the God of heaven and earth—the One who holds the universe by His own mighty power. The One who does according to His own will and none can withhold His hands to stop Him. Nor can anyone say to Him: "God, don't you think that's enough punishment and torment; why don't you stop?" "Oh God, I thought you were the God of love, have mercy on me!" Sorry, there is no mercy in hell, only vengeance and wrath.

Our duty is to warn the unsaved about this terrible place. If Jesus repeatedly warned about it, the church should do the same. But how are we to warn the people? Are we to speak our own words or the Word of God, the gospel?

CHAPTER 13

PREACHING IS THE APPOINTED MEANS OF THE PROCLAMATION OF THE GOSPEL

Romans 10:14: *How then shall they call on him in whom they have not believed? and how shall they believe in him of whom they have not heard? and how shall they hear without a preacher?*

Proclaiming the true gospel of Jesus Christ does not simply happen by quoting **John 3:16** or any other Bible verse to the unsaved. It is not enough to just say: "God loves you and that's why Jesus died for you." While that is true, it is not the full story. Just knowing that God loves you is not enough to save you.

One must come to terms with the reality of his own unimaginable sinfulness, the eternal judgment of God for those sins, and the eternal and most amazing price Jesus paid for those sins in averting the eternal judgment of God for all who will believe; a price that demands every sinner's attention. A gift that is worthy of all acceptation—never to be refused.

Unfortunately, most modern preaching does not give sinners an understanding of their great sinful wretchedness and urgent need of the Savior, Jesus Christ. As the Bible says, "Today if you hear His voice, do not harden your heart (**Hebrews 4:7**). Behold, now is the appointed time, now is the day of salvation" (**2 Corinthians 6:2**)—a very sober warning indeed to all sinners.

Preaching and quoting Bible verses are two different things. Preachers are supposed to study to show themselves approved unto God, rightly dividing the Word of truth. We are supposed to convince the hearers by sound doctrine, in order that they will come to the knowledge of the truth of Jesus Christ and be saved.

To accomplish this task, ministers must study the whole Bible: Old and

New Testaments, so that they can fully explain the gravity of sin and why Jesus had to die to pay for it. Sinners must understand that it's either Jesus or eternal judgment: no other choice and no other way to be saved.

Preachers are supposed to show men their absolute need of repentance and faith in Christ; that if they refuse Jesus, they will suffer severe eternal torments. That one day they will be judged for their sins, and there is no escape of God's eternal judgment.

Examples of true preaching are recorded in the book of Acts. When Peter and Paul preached the gospel, they didn't have **John 3:16** to preach, they had only the Old Testament Scriptures, and had to convince both Jews and Gentiles that all Scriptures pointed to the cross of Jesus Christ.

The apostles had to study the Scriptures to show that the cross was the absolute way of salvation and there was no other means. They had to truly defend their faith in Christ and give the reason for their hope in Him.

They had to prove that the Law proclaimed all guilty of sin and worthy of death and pointed to the grace of God in Christ; that keeping the Law could never save anyone. It was only given to reveal God's holiness and our sinfulness.

For example, Paul commended Timothy for adhering to the Old Testament Scriptures, which show the way of salvation by faith, which is in Jesus Christ:

2 Timothy 3:15: *And that from a child thou hast known the holy scriptures, which are able to make thee wise unto salvation through faith which is in Christ Jesus.*

Stephen and the Apostle Paul had to defend their reason for faith in Jesus Christ when the Jews accused them of heresy. Also, the Apostle Paul on many occasions had to fully explain the Old Testament

Scriptures in front of the elders of Israel and in front of kings in Jerusalem, Rome, and Asia, while undergoing persecution for allegedly preaching false doctrine against the Law of Moses. Stephen also gave his hope in Christ by expounding the Old Testament to the elders of Israel in **Acts chapter 8**, and even died as a result. He did not shy away from explaining that salvation is in Christ alone.

The Apostle Paul had to defend his life with Scriptures numerous times. He simply could not say to the people: "Jesus loves you and died to save you." They didn't all believe that; many of them thought they could be saved by the Law of Moses, and so rejected the grace of God in Christ.

Throughout the book of Acts, Paul had to fully expound the Scriptures, proving that Christ had to suffer and rise again the third day and that repentance and faith in Him were what all the prophets declared. He had to convince both Jews and Gentiles from the meticulous study of Scriptures. He wasn't a lazy preacher who told the people "Jesus died to save you because God loves you".

But now we are seeing a different kind of gospel that is very shallow when it comes to sin and repentance. It's all about how Jesus loves all people and died to bring them to heaven, without the mention of sin and repentance. They give the audience the impression that everything is well if you say a little prayer, without acknowledging why they are saying the prayer, and how serious the issue really is.

May I remind you that Jesus says in **Matthew 7** that many will profess to know Him, but He will say, "Depart from me all you workers of iniquity, I never knew you." In other words, if anyone claims to be saved, he must not continue in sin. He must follow righteousness. He must be born again and become a new creature made in the likeness of Christ.

Entertainment and story-telling were never the intended means by which the gospel was delivered. And that's what we are doing today. Instead, we are to go directly to Scriptures and preach them in their proper context. This includes studying the whole Bible to get the full meaning of what a passage is really saying.

The book of **Titus** tells us that God has manifested His word of eternal life through preaching:

Titus 1:2–3: *In hope of eternal life, which God, that cannot lie, promised before the world began; But hath in due times manifested his word through preaching, which is committed unto me according to the commandment of God our Saviour.*

God Himself made a marvelous statement about those who preach the gospel of good tidings. In the sight of God, it is the most wonderful job to perform! God ordained it that way!

Romans 10:15: *And how shall they preach, except they be sent? as it is written, How beautiful are the feet of them that preach the gospel of peace, and bring glad tidings of good things!*

Some will say that preaching is foolishness and will not want to hear it, but that's the method by which God chose to save sinners. God is well pleased by the method of preaching.

1 Corinthians 1:18: *For the preaching of the cross is to them that perish foolishness; but unto us which are saved it is the power of God.*

1 Corinthians 1:21: *For after that in the wisdom of God the world by wisdom knew not God, it pleased God by the foolishness of preaching to save them that believe.*

How did we get to this point where we have forgotten to preach the full gospel? We are preaching a gospel without sin and repentance. The gospel is very simple, but not easy to follow. We are making it so easy to follow when it could mean martyrdom for following Christ. Jesus says unless we deny ourselves and take up our cross daily, we cannot be His disciples.

It seems that ministers have forgotten that studying, applying, and preaching the Word of God is their main duty. Consequently, we seem to have forgotten what the gospel is all about and how we are to proclaim it. We forget that preaching is the appointed means of salvation.

It is evident, from what we are hearing in the churches these days, that preaching the Word in and out of season has been shoved aside for other forms of entertainment like storytelling and acting. Jesus appointed disciples to go and preach the kingdom of God, not storytelling and drama.

Matthew 10:7: *And as ye go, preach, saying, The kingdom of heaven is at hand.*

Mark 3:14: *And he ordained twelve, that they should be with him, and that he might send them forth to preach.*

Mark 6:12: *And they went out, and preached that men should repent.*

So, it is quite clear from Scriptures that preaching is the appointed means of the proclamation of the gospel. Many ministers today have not made this top priority, but have replaced it with other means of delivering the gospel such as storytelling and dramas. They have tried to take a shortcut to preaching by asking sinners to repeat "the sinners' prayer", which is not even the intended means of salvation.

Even though we have been commanded to preach the gospel, there is still a lot of confusion about what we should preach. The Bible clearly says that a person must be converted and be born again to enter heaven.

Furthermore, salvation is the gift of God through His effectual calling. In other words, if God does not call a person to Christ through His Holy Spirit, that person cannot come.

God gives salvation when He calls a person to repentance and faith in Christ through the conviction of the Holy Spirit. Salvation is really the work of God. It is not of man's free choice and ability to say, "yes or no" to Jesus that determines a person's salvation. **Romans 9** says that "it is not of him that willeth, but of God that sheweth mercy."

Romans 9:15–16: *For he saith to Moses, I will have mercy on whom I will have mercy, and I will have compassion on whom I will have compassion. So then it is not of him that willeth, nor of him that runneth, but of God that sheweth mercy.*

Now, if I tell a person to just repeat "the sinners' prayer", without that person being called and convicted by God through the Holy Spirit, that person cannot be converted. There will be no change in that person's life as required by God. The fruit of holiness will not be evident.

Repeating the "sinner's prayer" makes it seem as if salvation is in the sinner's hand, when in fact it's not. The sinner is dead in trespasses and sins and cannot respond to God without first being quickened by the Holy Spirit. In other words, you can't come to God unless He calls. That's why God says: "Today if you will hear is voice, harden not your heart" (**Hebrews 4:7**).

God opened the heart of Lydia to hear the gospel and be saved.

Acts 16:14: *And a certain woman named Lydia, a seller of purple, of the city of Thyatira, which worshipped God, heard us: whose heart the Lord opened, that she attended unto the things which were spoken of Paul.*

God told Cornelius to send for Apostle Peter to hear the gospel and be saved.

Acts 10:5-6: *And now send men to Joppa, and call for one Simon, whose surname is Peter. He lodgeth with one Simon a tanner, whose house is by the sea side: he shall tell thee what thou oughtest to do.*

God told the evangelist Philip to explain the gospel to the Ethiopian eunuch in order that he might be saved.

Acts 8:29–35 *Then the Spirit said unto Philip, Go near, and join thyself to this chariot. And Philip ran thither to him, and heard him read the prophet Esaias, and said, Understandest thou what thou readest? And he said, How can I, except some man should guide me? And he desired Philip that he would come up and sit with him. The place of the scripture which he read was this, He was led as a sheep to the* *slaughter; and like a lamb dumb before his shearer, so opened he not his mouth: In his humiliation his judgment was taken away: and who shall declare his generation? for his life is taken from the earth. And the eunuch answered Philip, and said, I pray thee, of whom speaketh the prophet this? of himself, or of some other man? Then Philip opened his mouth, and began at the same scripture, and preached unto him Jesus.*

The Apostle Peter says the promise of salvation is to as many as the Lord shall call:

Acts 2:39: *For the promise is unto you, and to your children, and to all that are afar off, even as many as the Lord our God shall call.*

1 Corinthians 1:26: *For ye see your calling, brethren, how that not many wise men after the flesh, not many mighty, not many noble, are called.*

CHAPTER 14

THE ELEVATION OF TONGUES ABOVE OTHER GIFTS OF THE SPIRIT, LIKE PROPHECY

Is speaking in tongues the only true sign of the Baptism or filling of the Holy Ghost?

Is it an absolute requirement that a person speak in tongues as the main sign of conversion?

The issue of speaking in tongues has become a big topic for the church today when it should not be. Some seem to confuse the filling of the Spirit with the Baptism. This subject has caused a lot of confusion and divisions. It seems to have taken precedence above other gifts of the Spirit.

Pentecostals seem to use the event that happened on the day of Pentecost as the model for the baptism of the Holy Spirit, claiming that all who are baptized by the Holy Spirit must speak in tongues. But is that the only sign that a person has been given the Holy Spirit?

Acts 2:4: *And they were all* ***filled*** *with the Holy Ghost, and began to speak with other tongues, as the Spirit gave them utterance.*

First, the Bible does not say that the people in the book of **Acts** spoke in tongues on the day of Pentecost because they were baptized in the Spirit; it says they were filled with the Spirit and began to speak with other tongues. Why is it then that we always make the claim that they were baptized with the Spirit?

There was a specific reason why they all spoke in tongues on the day of Pentecost. But we have missed the real reason. It was a sign to the Jews. God wanted all the Jews to know that Jesus Christ, whom they rejected and crucified, was their long-awaited Messiah, their Savior. The shocking truth to the Jews was that the one they hated and crucified without a cause was indeed the one Moses and the prophets wrote about.

The day of Pentecost was God-ordained. It was called the Feast of Weeks (*Shavuot*), and in the Old Testament, was originally an agricultural festival celebrating and giving thanks for the "first fruits" of the early spring harvest (**Leviticus 23, Exodus 23, 34**). (This festival is a picture of the resurrection of Christ, the first fruits—**1 Corinthians 15:20.**)

God already knew that Jews from every nation would be gathered on the day of Pentecost, and so He wanted them to know that Jesus who was crucified and resurrected is both Lord and Christ. God spoke to the house of Israel to let them know that the One they rejected was really their Lord, King, and Savior.

The Jews still would not believe in Jesus after all the signs and wonders they had seen, as was also foretold. As Isaiah prophesied, "For all this, still they will not hear because they hardened their hearts and closed their eyes, lest they should see with their eyes, and hear with their ears, and understand with their heart, and should be converted, and I should heal them" (**Isaiah 6:9**).

At the end of Peter's sermon in **Acts 2**, he pointed out that the miracle of speaking in tongues in the native languages of the Jews was a sign to all the house of Israel (Jews), that this same Jesus they crucified was the Messiah spoken of by the Law and prophets, and that all sinners (Jews and Gentiles) must come through Him to be saved. He further warned them that salvation is in no other name but the name of Jesus; that Jesus could not be avoided if they wanted to enter the kingdom of God.

Acts 2:36: *Therefore let all the house of Israel know assuredly, that God hath made that same Jesus, whom ye have crucified, both Lord and Christ.*

The event of speaking in tongues that took place on the day of Pentecost was what God promised He would do to the house of Israel. God promised in the book of Isaiah that He would speak to them with stammering lips and other tongues, but they would not hear. That's exactly what He did on the day of Pentecost.

Isaiah 28:11: *For with stammering lips and another tongue will he speak to this people.*

But you ask: didn't two other groups in the book of Acts also all speak in tongues, proving that speaking in tongues is the ultimate sign of the manifestation of the Spirit? (The two groups were: Cornelius and his household, and the twelve believers baptized unto John's baptism for the repentance and remission of sins.)

First, salvation was promised to the world by the Messiah through the nation of Israel, and that's what was fulfilled on the day of Pentecost. But the Jews did not know that the Gentiles would also be partakers of the promise, and so before God gave the Holy Spirit to Cornelius and his household, He sent for Peter (Jew).

The Jews despised the Gentiles and thought only they were children of the kingdom of God. God wanted the Jews to know that the Gentiles also were given salvation. As was promised in **Isaiah 49:6**, the Messiah would be a light to the Gentiles.

The Apostle Paul repeatedly explains this mystery of Jews and Gentiles being of the same body of Christ in his epistles:

Ephesians 3:4–6: *Whereby, when ye read, ye may understand my knowledge in the mystery of Christ) Which in other ages was not made known unto the sons of men, as it is now revealed unto his holy apostles and prophets by the Spirit; That the Gentiles should be fellowheirs, and of the same body, and partakers of his promise in Christ by the gospel.*

Colossians 1:27*: To whom God would make known what is the riches of the glory of this mystery among the Gentiles; which is Christ in you, the hope of glory.*

The grafting in of the Gentiles into the olive tree (Israel) was not known by the Jews, and so God made it known to them, using the Apostle Peter.

This story is given in **Acts 10**, and it tells us that Peter had a vision of a vessel coming down from heaven knit at the four corners with all kinds of unclean animals. God then commanded Peter to eat, but he refused, because they were unclean. God explained the vision and told Peter that what He has cleansed (Gentiles) to not call common or unclean. This was a vision for Peter to go preach to the Gentile Cornelius.

While Peter preached the gospel to Cornelius, the Holy Spirit fell on Cornelius and his household. God was the one who gave the Holy Spirit to these Gentiles so that Peter could testify to the rest of the Jews that God made no difference between any nation, whether Jew or Gentile; that God gave the Gentiles the same gift He gave them. This was a surprise to Peter, and he had to make a defense to his fellow Jews why he went to a Gentile's house.

Acts 10:44–46: *While Peter yet spake these words, the Holy Ghost fell on all them which heard the word. And they of the circumcision which believed were astonished, as many as came with Peter, because that on the Gentiles also was poured out the gift of the Holy Ghost. For they heard them speak with tongues, and magnify God…*

Also, when Jesus warned the Jews that He was going to a place they could not go, they asked if he were going to be among the Gentiles and teach them, showing their animosity towards the Gentiles:

John 7:35: *Then said the Jews among themselves, Whither will he go, that we shall not find him? will he go unto the dispersed among the Gentiles, and teach the Gentiles?*

This other group (Gentiles) all spoke in tongues as a sign to the Jews that the Gentiles were also part of the kingdom of God. It was so ordained by God. It was God who spoke to both Peter and Cornelius in a vision to set up this meeting between a Jew and Gentile.

Peter was the witness that, through Jesus Christ, the Gentiles had become a part of one family in the household of God; there is no difference between Jews and Gentiles. The sign of tongues was a visible manifestation that Gentiles were also reconciled to God, which the Jews could not deny, because they were the first recipients and witnesses.

Another group which all spoke in tongues and prophesied was the twelve believers in **Acts 19**. You will notice that this group were baptized unto John's baptism of repentance for the remission of sins. Paul asked them if they had received the Holy Ghost, but they said they never heard of Him.

The Apostle Paul then preached to them Jesus and they believed. He then laid His hands on them to receive the Holy Ghost and baptized them in the name of Jesus. They all spoke in tongues and prophesied, as the sign confirming Jesus as the One John the Baptist said would come after him and baptize with the Holy Spirit.

After it was established by the sign of speaking in tongues that Jesus is the Savior of all men, Jews and Gentiles, no matter the race or nationality, we see in **1 Corinthians 14** that not all who are already saved and baptized into the body of Christ by the Spirit, speak in tongues.

1Corinthians 12:30: *Have all the gifts of healing? do all speak with tongues? do all interpret?*

The Apostle Paul explains that the Spirit gives different spiritual gifts, and not all have the gift of tongues. But we are commanded to pursue the gift of prophecy because that's really the will of God: God promised in **Joel 2** that He would pour out His Spirit and we would prophesy; He didn't promise we would speak in tongues, He promised we would prophesy.

1 Corinthians 14:1: *Follow after charity, and desire spiritual gifts, but rather that ye may prophesy.*

1 Corinthians 14:22–25: *Wherefore tongues are for a sign, not to them that believe, but to them that believe not: but prophesying serveth not for them that believe not, but for them which believe. If therefore the whole church be come together into one* *place, and all speak with tongues, and there come in those that are unlearned, or unbelievers, will they not say that ye are mad? But if all prophesy, and there come in one that believeth not, or one unlearned, he is convinced of all, he is judged of all: And thus are the secrets of his heart made manifest; and so falling down on his face he will worship God, and report that God is in you of a truth.*

Joel 2:28: *And it shall come to pass afterward, that I will pour out my spirit upon all flesh; and your sons and your daughters shall prophesy, your old men shall dream dreams, your young men shall see visions.*

In the Old Testament, for example, when the Holy Spirit came upon Saul, he prophesied:

1 Samuel 10:10: *And when they came thither to the hill, behold, a company of prophets met him; and the Spirit of God came upon him, and he prophesied among them.*

Also, God gave the Spirit to the seventy elders of Israel and they also prophesied:

Numbers 11:25: *And the LORD came down in a cloud, and spake unto him, and took of the spirit that was upon him, and gave it unto the seventy elders: and it came to pass, that, when the spirit rested upon them, they prophesied, and did not cease.*

The Apostle Paul also explains this misuse of tongues in **1 Corinthians 14**. He says greater is he who prophesies than he who speaks in tongues. God wants to edify His church through prophesying. But Pentecostals have placed more emphasis on tongues, and that's the problem.

The Apostle Paul did not forbid the use of tongues. What he says is that when we come together, then let there be order with the use of tongues. If we all start speaking in tongues without interpretation, then we are like children in our understanding (**1 Corinthians 14:20**).

We are commanded to be with understanding like men and to know the use of tongues and prophesying. If not, we will neglect the most important part of spiritual gifts, which is to edify the church in a language they all understand so that they can all say, Amen.

In summary, showing our spirituality by speaking in tongues is not even the main point of the new life in Christ; it is living a holy life. What a tragedy it would be to have spoken in tongues and prophesied all our lives just to hear on the day of Christ, "Depart from me you workers of iniquity" (**Matthew 7:23**). Let us focus on the most important aspect of the Christian life, "Be holy for I am holy" (**1 Peter 1:16**), says the Lord, and God will pour out His Spirit on us, no doubt.

It is a common fact that some will not agree with the things I agree with, and vice versa. That's just the way it is. We all don't know everything in the Bible, but some things are made plain to us, and tongues is one of those things. I am always learning and make mistakes myself. So, if there is any doctrine that I have gone astray with, please correct me and show me from Scriptures the truth.

Now that I have discussed some divisive issues in the church by explaining, as I see in Scriptures, certain doctrines that have caused confusion and diversion from the true gospel, such as tongues, Sabbath day, meat, the Law, etc., let us move forward into the real essence of the gospel.

Preaching is necessary for salvation

As we should know, as demonstrated in scriptures, preaching is the appointed means God made for the deliverance of the gospel. But what exactly are we to preach? Should we just say to the unsaved: Jesus loves you and that's why He died for you? Is that what the apostles preached? Is that what John the Baptist and Jesus preached?

Even though God created all men and loves them, this does not mean all will go to heaven just because God loves them. The reason being, we were born in sin, and the Bible declares in **1 Corinthians 15:50**, "flesh and blood (sinful flesh), cannot inherit the kingdom of God." One must repent, believe the gospel, and be born again of the Spirit of God

John 3:3: *Jesus answered and said unto him, Verily, verily, I say unto thee, Except a man be born again, he cannot see the kingdom of God.*

John 1:12–13: *But as many as received him, to them gave he power to become the sons of God, even to them that believe on his name: Which were born, not of blood, nor of the will of the flesh, nor of the will of man, but of God.*

A preacher then must explain the full context of the Bible, showing sinners from the Old Testament the seriousness of sin because of the fall of Adam, the terrible eternal judgment for sin, and the mercy (cross of Jesus Christ) that God has provided as a ransom (payment) to redeem us back to God.

Upon hearing the full counsel of the gospel, the fear of the judgment of God must fall upon sinners to bring them to the cross. Otherwise, they will not tremble before God and repent of their sins and follow Christ. Don't just say "Jesus loves you and died for you"; that does not bring the fear of God.

CHAPTER 15

PROSPERITY GOSPEL: THE MISREPRESENTATION OF TRUE WEALTH IN CHRIST

2 Corinthians 8:9: *For ye know the grace of our Lord Jesus Christ, that, though he was rich, yet for your sakes he became poor, that ye through his poverty might be rich.*

Looking at this Scripture, many "Christians" are tempted to believe that Jesus became poor to make us financial wealthy in this life. While we are joint-heirs with Christ and will inherit all that God has in this universe, God did not promise us riches in this life, but trials and tribulations until we see Jesus. He promised that we will reign and rule with Christ if we suffer with Him.

But many false teachers are misusing these Scriptures for their own financial profit. They are fulfilling exactly what the Apostle Peter prophesied in **2 Peter**, which states that this practice will result in their swift and severe destruction by Almighty God. Financial wealth is not part of the gospel, neither was it ever promised by God as part of the blessings of salvation in Christ.

2 Peter 2:1–3: *But there were false prophets also among the people, even as there shall be false teachers among you, who privily shall bring in damnable heresies, even denying the Lord that bought them, and bring upon themselves swift destruction. And many shall follow their pernicious ways; by reason of whom the way of truth shall be evil spoken of. And through covetousness shall they with feigned words make merchandise of you: whose judgment now of a long time lingereth not, and their damnation slumbereth not.*

We are told in the book of **Ephesians** that God has blessed us with all spiritual blessings in Christ. It doesn't mention anything about financial wealth like the millionaires and billionaires of this world. But since money is such a big force in this world, the Bible does say a lot about it, but contrary to what many might believe.

The world considers the rich greatly blessed. On the other hand, the poor, rich in faith, are considered rich by God. Therefore, God's view of wealth and the world's view of wealth are in opposition.

Ephesians 1:3: *Blessed be the God and Father of our Lord Jesus Christ, who hath blessed us with all spiritual blessings in heavenly places in Christ.*

Financial prosperity has totally corrupted the gospel message and is leading many away from the true gospel. We often hear preachers quoting Old Testament Scriptures such as **Deuteronomy 28:1–9** as prosperity blessings promised by God, but they are only using these verses for their own profit. In addition, many are also teaching that the blessing of Abraham (material wealth) has been given to us in Jesus Christ.

This all sounds wonderful, but is it true that all believers are to be wealthy? Is this what the Bible says, or is this man's opinion to fulfill and justify their carnal desire? If that's the case, why did the Apostle Paul suffer hunger, distresses, and persecutions? Why did he thank the Philippian church for supplying his needs?

If all Christians were supposed to always have more than enough, why was the Apostle Paul in need, seeing he was the greatest apostle of the Lord? Didn't the Apostle Paul receive the blessings of Abraham?

The Bible tells us that we have received the blessing of Abraham through Jesus Christ, the seed of Abraham; that blessing is the gift of the Holy Spirit, not material possessions.

Galatians 3:13–14: *Christ hath redeemed us from the curse of the law, being made a curse for us: for it is written, Cursed is every one that hangeth on a tree: That the blessing of Abraham might come on the Gentiles through Jesus Christ; that we might receive the promise of the* ***Spirit*** *through faith.* Also, we see in numerous Scriptures that the true blessing of God is the forgiveness of sins.

Romans 4:7–8: *Saying, Blessed are they whose iniquities are forgiven, and whose sins are covered. Blessed is the man to whom the Lord will not impute sin.*

When the Apostle Peter preached on the day of Pentecost, he preached that the blessing of God was the forgiveness of sins through His Son Jesus Christ.

Acts 3:26: *Unto you first God, having raised up his Son Jesus, sent him to **bless** you, in turning away every one of you from his iniquities.*

We are also reminded in **James 2:5** that God has chosen the poor of this world, rich in faith to be heirs of His kingdom. Furthermore, the Apostle Paul said that they were poor, yet making many rich. Why did he also say that even though he possessed nothing, he possessed all things? He was talking about being spiritually rich in Christ, not in temporal material things.

2 Corinthians 6:10: *As sorrowful, yet alway rejoicing; as poor, yet making many rich; as having nothing, and yet possessing all things.*

The Apostle Paul took offerings from the churches in Macedonia and Achaia for the poor saints in Jerusalem. That's another reason why tithes and offerings are given; that those who have nothing may have something, that there will be no lack in the body of Christ.

God has already supplied everything to His church. Some are rich, while others are poor. The rich are supposed to distribute to the poor.

Romans 15:26: *For it hath pleased them of Macedonia and Achaia to make a certain contribution for the poor saints which are at Jerusalem.*

Not everyone can handle financial wealth in a way that glorifies God. So, God knows exactly why He must keep riches from some of us. He does it to save us from ruin that results from being led away from the faith. The poor, as stated in **Zephaniah 3:12** and **1 Timothy 5:5**, put their trust in God. God wants us to put our trust in Him and to totally depend on Him for everything.

Zephaniah 3:12: *I will also leave in the midst of thee an afflicted and poor people, and they shall trust in the name of the* LORD.

1 Timothy 5:5: *Now she that is a widow indeed, and desolate, trusteth in God, and continueth in supplications and prayers night and day.*

We also see in the book of Revelation that Jesus commends the church in Smyrna, not because they were materially wealthy, but spiritually rich. In fact, they were quite poor. They had suffered much tribulation and deep poverty, but Jesus said they were rich. Their situations compelled them to fully trust in Him as their Healer, Deliverer, Shepherd, and Provider; Jesus was their full sufficiency in all things; their all in all.

Revelation 2:9: *I know thy works, and tribulation, and poverty, (but thou art rich) and I know the blasphemy of them which say they are Jews, and are not, but are the synagogue of Satan.*

In contrast, He told the Laodiceans that they were lukewarm and needed to repent, because they had increased in goods and thought they were rich, when in fact they were poor, spiritually, in the sight of God.

Revelation 3:17: *Because thou sayest, I am rich, and increased with goods, and have need of nothing; and knowest not that thou art wretched, and miserable, and poor, and blind, and naked.*

So, what are true riches, if it is not being financially wealthy?

As described in the verse below, possessing true riches means having a faith tested in the fire, being fully covered in the righteousness of Christ, and having eyes that can see clearly.

Revelation 3:18: *I counsel thee to buy of me gold tried in the fire, that* **thou mayest be rich**; *and white raiment, that thou mayest be clothed, and that the shame of thy nakedness do not appear; and anoint thine eyes with eyesalve, that thou mayest see.*

This might not sound great to many, but God's ways are not like ours. What am I saying? I am saying that having eyes focused on material wealth leads to destruction. The doctrine of the gospel is according to godliness (**1 Timothy 6: 3**).

These are some of the reasons why a focus on material wealth (prosperity gospel) is very destructive.

God has promised to leave a poor and afflicted people in order that they will trust in Him.

Zephaniah 3:12: *I will also leave in the midst of thee an afflicted and poor people, and they shall trust in the name of the LORD.*

If Christians always have a surplus always, then they will not trust in the Lord; they will trust in their money.

The book of Proverbs has much to say about riches, and it's not good!

Proverbs 11:28: *He that trusteth in his riches shall fall: but the righteous shall flourish as a branch.*

Proverbs 13:7: *There is that maketh himself rich, yet hath nothing: there is that maketh himself poor, yet hath great riches.*

Proverbs 11:4: *Riches profit not in the day of wrath: but righteousness delivereth from death.*

Proverbs 28:22: *He that hasteth to be rich hath an evil eye, and considereth not that poverty shall come upon him.*

As you can see, riches will not profit in the day of wrath, but righteousness will deliver souls from eternal death. Also, he who is eager to get rich has an evil eye.

The love of money is the root of all evil and causes many to stray from the faith to the path that leads to destruction. Also, those that are rich fall into temptation and a snare. It is a very subtle and deadly trap.

1 Timothy 6:9–10: *But they that will be rich fall into temptation and a snare, and into many foolish and hurtful lusts, which drown men in destruction and* *perdition. For the love of money is the root of all evil: which while some coveted after, they have erred from the faith, and pierced themselves through with many sorrows.*

Jesus said that the poor would always be in the land (**Matthew 26:11**). In other words, there is a reason for this. On the Day of Judgment, Jesus will separate the goats from the sheep. He will say to those on His right hand, "I was hungry and you gave me meat". He will then say to those on His left hand, "I was hungry and you gave me no meat" (**Matthew 25:33–46**).

Some Christians will be poor for allowing other Christians (brothers and sisters in Christ) to minister to them. Ministering to poor, naked, and hungry Christians is ministering to the Lord. That's how Christians get opportunities to show their love to the Lord. When we minister to Christians in their need, we are ministering to Christ through them.

Matthew 25:40: *And the King shall answer and say unto them, Verily I say unto you, Inasmuch as ye have done it unto one of the least of these my brethren, ye have done it unto me.*

Proverbs 19:17: *He that hath pity upon the poor lendeth unto the LORD; and that which he hath given will he pay him again.*

Do you remember when the Apostle Paul (Saul) was persecuting Christians? What did Jesus say to him? Jesus told the Apostle Paul that he was persecuting Him (Jesus) when he persecuted the Christians. Don't forget, Christians are the body of Christ.

CHAPTER 16

SODOMY (HOMOSEXUALITY) IS SIN AND IS AN ABOMINATION: THE BIBLE STRONGLY CONDEMNS IT

This topic of same-sex partners/marriage has become a big issue today, from which arise constant debates on whether homosexuality is acceptable by God. Some pastors and priests are teaching that there is nothing wrong with being a sodomite because that's the way God made them.

Well, it's quite clear in the Bible that all of us are sinners who need to repent and believe in Jesus Christ to be saved from our own sins; homosexuality is listed as one of those sins and is an abominable one.

Leviticus 18:22: *Thou shalt not lie with mankind, as with womankind: it is abomination.*

Leviticus 20:13: *If a man also lie with mankind, as he lieth with a woman, both of them have committed an abomination: they shall surely be put to death; their blood shall be upon them.*

It is listed in the Old Testament as an abominable sin. The New Testament reiterates this point by saying no homosexuals can enter heaven.

1 Corinthians 6:9: *Know ye not that the unrighteous shall not inherit the kingdom of God? Be not deceived: neither fornicators, nor idolaters, nor adulterers, nor effeminate, nor abusers of themselves with mankind.*

In the last book of the Bible, the book of Revelation, it clearly shows that the abominable (a man who lies with another man), will have their part in the lake of fire.

Revelation 21:8: *But the fearful, and unbelieving, and the abominable, and murderers, and whoremongers, and sorcerers, and idolaters, and all liars, shall have* *their part in the lake which burneth with fire and brimstone: which is the second death.*

With so many Scriptures from the Old and New testaments showing that having sex with someone of the same gender is an abomination, and against the will of God and is very sinful, how can anyone say it is not a sin and is therefore acceptable by God?

Well, some are still not satisfied with the evidence of Scriptures and will try to twist the Word of God to conform to their sinful lifestyle, but that will not work with God. God does not conform to any sinner. He commands all sinners to repent. God has spoken repeatedly of this sin, but they will not listen.

Many will even go as far as to say Jesus did not mention anything about same-sex relationships. How much more do you want Jesus to say to agree with your sin? The Pharisees questioned Jesus about marriage and divorce, and Jesus said, "from the beginning of creation God made them male and female." Now, what do you think Jesus meant when He referred to marriage as a union between a male and female? Jesus doesn't have to say any more.

Mark 10:6: *But from the beginning of the creation God made them male and female.*

Why are people still blinded by the practice of sodomy? I chose purposely the word "Sodomite" because of its relation to the cities of Sodom and Gomorrah, which God destroyed for practicing this sin. Sodomite is the proper word because it is linked with the judgment of God upon the city of Sodom.

Those who will not see that homosexuality is sin have rejected the truth of God, and as a result, God has given them over to the lust of their own heart to practice what they so desire: homosexuality.

Romans 1:26–28: *For this cause God gave them up unto vile affections: for even their women did change the natural use into that which is against nature: And* *likewise also the men, leaving the natural use of the woman, burned in their lust one toward another; men with men working that which is unseemly, and receiving in themselves that recompence of their error which was meet. And even as they did not like to retain God in their knowledge, God gave them over to a reprobate mind, to do those things which are not convenient.*

What the sodomites are not aware of is that they have rejected the truth of God, and God has given them over to this sin. Consequently, for their error, they have received their due reward: whatever sickness or diseases are associated with it.

It should be obvious by our God-given conscience that a marriage relationship should be between a man and woman. The problem is that those who insist that it's not wrong to practice sodomy have defiled their conscience and have taken what is wrong and made it right in their own sight, which is against nature and God's purpose and will.

CHAPTER 17

GOSPEL FACTS

When it comes to the gospel, there are essential facts that we must know for us to declare the full counsel of God with authority. Very essential to the gospel, is the person of Jesus Christ. It is all about Him. Some will say that they believe He is the Son of God, but they won't say that He is God the Creator, the Almighty God, the Alpha and Omega. Please note: Jesus Christ is not someone you can ever fully explain, because He is God.

So, here are some very important truths declared in the Bible, regarding the person of Jesus Christ and what the gospel is:

The gospel to be preached:

The gospel is not of man but of God. **Galatians 1:11–12**

The gospel is the good news of the kingdom of God and not about this earthly kingdom. **Matthew 9:35**

We are to preach Jesus Christ, His death, burial, and resurrection. **1 Corinthians 15:1–4**

The Lord Jesus Christ gave Himself for our sins to deliver us from this present evil world according to the will of God the Father. **Galatians 1:4**

Jesus Christ is the righteousness of God revealed from heaven; He is the power of God unto salvation for everyone who believes. **Romans 1:16–17**

Christ crucified is the main point. **1 Corinthians 1:23**

Jesus is the only Savior. **Acts 4:12**

The gospel is the grace of God. **Acts 20:24**

We are saved by grace through faith in Christ alone, not by works of the

Law. **Ephesians 2:8–9**

Jesus was the only just payment for sins that satisfied God's perfect justice. **Romans 3:25–26**

The truth is according to godliness. **Titus 1:1**

Jesus is the judge of all men. **Romans 2:16**

Every knee will bow and every tongue will confess that Jesus is Lord. **Philippians 2:11**

Jesus is God, the Creator. **Colossians 1:15**

He who believes in Jesus Christ is not condemned. **John 3:18**

He who does not believe in Jesus Christ is condemned already. **John 3:18**

Repent for the kingdom of heaven is at hand. **Matthew 4:17**

Repent and be converted. **Acts 3:19**

It is not easy to enter heaven; you enter the kingdom of God through much tribulation. **Acts 14:22**

If you live godly, you will suffer persecution. **2 Timothy 3:12**

You must be born again to enter heaven. **John 3:3**

You must deny yourself, take up your cross and follow Jesus. **Luke 9:23**

Jesus is God who became a man to redeem sinners. **Philippians 2:5–8**

Jesus is the only way to God. **John 14:6**

It is impossible to know God without Jesus; He is God the Son who reveals the Father. **Matthew 11:27**

Jesus calls His sheep

We have heard it preached repeatedly that we should believe in Jesus and ask Him into our heart, and we will be saved. This makes salvation sound very easy, because this decision to choose Jesus is really in the sinner's hand. This is contrary to the Bible.

First, we don't get to choose Jesus; He is the one who does the choosing, and He does not choose everyone. He calls His sheep through the Holy Spirit. He knows His sheep: those He has chosen. That's the reason why asking Jesus into your heart and saying the sinners' prayer is against the gospel.

John 15:16: *Ye have not chosen me, but I have chosen you, and ordained you, that ye should go and bring forth fruit, and that your fruit should remain: that whatsoever ye shall ask of the Father in my name, he may give it you.*

John 6:44: *No man can come to me, except the Father which hath sent me draw him: and I will raise him up at the last day.*

Jesus says some people will not believe in Him because they are not His sheep and He did not choose them.

John 10:26: *But ye believe not, because ye are not of my sheep, as I said unto you.*

John 13:18: *I speak not of you all: I know whom I have chosen: but that the scripture may be fulfilled, He that eateth bread with me hath lifted up his heel against me.*

To believe and trust in Jesus as Savior and Lord is to repent of your sins, take up your cross, deny yourself and follow Him: your life is committed to Him and not to yourself. The result of believing in Jesus is a changed life that shows fruits of holiness and righteousness, and has zeal for the things of God.

Jesus calls us to holiness. He makes us into children of God who follow righteousness. If we are not born again, but instead choose to follow the religion of Christianity by trying to live a moral life based on the Sermon on the Mount, we are still children of the Devil and cannot enter heaven.

If we are only told to only say a prayer, asking Jesus into our heart without showing any signs of the new life of holiness and righteousness, then Jesus will say to those fake, unconverted Christians: "Depart from me you workers of iniquity, I never knew you" (**Matthew 7:23**).

Essential truths of the glorious gospel:

The gospel was the mystery kept secret since the foundation of the world. **Rom. 16:25**

It testifies that God was in Christ reconciling the world unto Himself. **2 Cor. 5:19**

The Holy Ghost was sent down from heaven to explain the gospel. **1 Pet. 1:11–12**

The gospel is glorious. **1 Tim. 1:11**

The gospel brings life and immortality through the death, burial, and resurrection of Jesus Christ. **2 Tim. 1:10**

The gospel is the Word of God that endures forever. **1 Peter 1:25**

The gospel was preached before to Abraham. **Gal. 3:8**

CHAPTER 18

GIVING IS ESSENTIAL TO THE CHRISTIAN LIFE, AND FOR THE WORK OF GOD TO CONTINUE

Under the Old Testament, giving was essential to the work of God. It provided God's house with everything necessary for the ministers of God to do what God commanded them to do. This giving was always done by the people of God. Whatever God has given to His people financially, they are to give a portion back to their Father's house, so that the work of their Father can be done without delay.

Malachi 3:10: *Bring ye all the tithes into the storehouse, that there may be meat in mine house, and prove me now herewith, saith the LORD of hosts, if I will not open you the windows of heaven, and pour you out a blessing, that there shall not be room enough to receive it.*

Tithing/giving is very important because when we give, God also gives us more grace to abound in our spiritual walk. Giving allows us to grow more and more into the stature of Christ. Many of us are not growing in grace because we don't give. Giving is love in action and is the summation of the gospel.

The church does not like to teach about giving or tithing because many will become offended. Giving is very important because that's what the gospel is based on. **John 3:16** tells us that God so loved the world that He gave His only begotten Son to die for us. Giving was a demonstration of God's sacrificial love for us. For this reason, we are to do the same.

The reason why we become offended when tithing or giving is mentioned in the church is because we have made money our god. We forget that we are only stewards of the financial blessing that God has given us and that everything belongs to Him. It is God who gave us the power and strength to gain wealth.

As a result, we are commanded to give to those who are in need. This means we are supposed to also give sacrificially. If God gave the life of His Only Son, why should we hold back on giving money? Is money more important than life?

Tithing is a very important part of the gospel and should be taught by the church even though many will be offended. There are numerous blessings given by God when a Christian faithfully and cheerfully gives. Not only does tithing supply the necessities of other believers, it is a form of thanksgiving to God, acknowledging that He is the source of all good things.

Matthew 5:42: *Give to him that asketh thee, and from him that would borrow of thee turn not thou away.*

2 Corinthians 9:7–13: *Every man according as he purposeth in his heart, so let him give; not grudgingly, or of necessity: for God loveth a cheerful giver. And God is able to make all grace abound toward you; that ye, always having all sufficiency in all things, may abound to every good work: (As it is written, He hath dispersed abroad; he hath given to the poor: his righteousness remaineth for ever. Now he that ministereth seed to the sower both minister bread for your food, and multiply your seed sown, and increase the fruits of your righteousness;) Being enriched in every thing to all bountifulness, which causeth through us thanksgiving to God. For the administration of this service not only supplieth the want of the saints, but is abundant also by many thanksgivings unto God; Whiles by the experiment of this ministration they glorify God for your professed subjection unto the gospel of Christ, and for your liberal distribution unto them, and unto all men.*

Could it be that many of us are struggling in many areas of our lives because we don't like to give? According to the Scriptures, when we tithe/give, we are the ones who receive many benefits. Giving is the gospel itself. We are told that God first gave us His only begotten Son and that we should also give freely to anyone who asks of us.

As explained in **2 Corinthians 9**, when we give, giving:

1. Is an expression of Love for God.

2. Supplies the necessities of the saints.
3. Shows obedience to the gospel of Christ.
4. Is an expression of thanksgiving to God.

In return, God does the following:

1. God makes all grace abound in everything.
2. God multiplies the seed sown.
3. God increases the fruits of your righteousness.
4. God gives sufficiency in all things.
5. God makes you abound in every good work.

In short, God blesses you, not only financially, but also in every area of your life because of cheerful giving, because giving shows obedience and love for God, our fellow brothers and sisters in Christ, and obedience to the gospel of Christ.

Why don't we respond to tithing the same way we respond to other doctrines of the Bible?

The pastor can preach about the love of God, but he knows that the minute he starts talking about money, we get offended. While it is true that there are many wolves in sheep's clothing who want to get rich by using tithing as the means, we should not rule out tithing altogether because of that. We should be aware of these wolves, but continue to support the true work of God.

We hold back on giving because we have made money our god. It is an indication that our mind is not fully set on the kingdom of God, but on self. I confess to this sin, and am no exception. It is the fleshly and sinful man that needs to be put down, which is a constant battle on this side of eternity.

Refusing to give to the kingdom of God sacrificially is an indication that we really don't have the love of God, or the love we have is not perfected. I believe it shows that the depth of our knowledge of the love of Christ, as demonstrated on the cross, is not as deep as it should be. Jesus gave everything He could ever give to us: His own life. How can we respond in our giving? We can never come close to what Christ gave to us! We all fall miserably short! We praise Him for His grace and mercy!

Giving money is the easy part. We are commanded to give our lives for the brethren. Which would you rather do? Give money or give your life?

God did not give us a command that He Himself did not do. Although He had nothing to prove, since He is the giver of life to all living things, He laid down His life for us to demonstrate His love. If God did that for us, shouldn't we do the same for our brethren?

But would we really want to give our lives for our brethren? This really shows how amazing God's mercy towards us is and how sinful we are. The fact is we don't like to give sacrificially and we also don't like to give our lives for the brethren.

Despite our failures, God still chooses to love us greatly. Praise His awesome and holy name for all He has done! If we could only see ourselves in contrast to the love of God for us who are in Christ, then we would really understand why God truly deserves all the glory for His grace. "Holy Father, I ask you to open our eyes to understand the glory of your grace, in Jesus' name, Amen."

1 John 3:16: *Hereby perceive we the love of God, because he laid down his life for us: and we ought to lay down our lives for the brethren.*

The Apostle Paul commends the Philippian Christians for providing his necessities and reminds them that whenever they give, God adds fruit to their account. In other words, it is a sign of fruit-bearing that will last forever:

Philippians 4:15–17: *Now ye Philippians know also, that in the beginning of the gospel, when I departed from Macedonia, no church communicated with me as concerning giving and receiving, but ye only. For even in Thessalonica ye sent once and again unto my necessity. Not because I desire a gift: but I desire fruit that may abound to your account.*

How can we perform this kind of giving that is contrary to our sinful flesh? Only when Christ can flow through a believer, can giving become a form of thanksgiving to God, and not just a religious activity to be performed.

We first should abide in the vine, Christ, so that He can flow through us: we need to surrender everything to Jesus and truly follow Him. Then He will do His work in us. This kind of giving is the work of the Holy Spirit and is a very necessary part of the gospel of Christ.

Giving is very important so that the work of God can be carried out. We are entrusted with the proclamation of the gospel, and that's done through prayer and financial support. How can we go to other cities and countries to preach the gospel if we don't have the money to do it?

CHAPTER 19

JESUS IS THE BUILDER AND FOUNDATION OF HIS CHURCH

Matthew 16:18: *And I say also unto thee, That thou art Peter, and upon this rock I will build my church; and the gates of hell shall not prevail against it.*

Colossians 1:18: *And he is the head of the body, the church: who is the beginning, the firstborn from the dead; that in all things he might have the preeminence.*

The Church that Jesus is building is built on the foundation of the Word of God and administered by Christ as the Head.

In most churches today, the Word of God does not seem to be the foundation by which they stand. The cross of Christ does not seem to be the focus. We have become "seeker sensitive". The only problem with this "seeker-sensitive method" is that no one seeks after God. And if they are seeking, it's because God is drawing them to Himself. There is none who seeks after God, says **Romans 3:10–11**. Jesus says no one can come to Him unless the Father draws him (**John 6:44**).

Now, if the Father is drawing someone to Jesus, why then do we must be sensitive to their feelings by not preaching the full gospel: the part about sin, judgment, and hell? Remember, when God draws people to Himself, He is bringing them to a place of repentance by showing them their sins and the judgment they deserve.

So then, those God is drawing will have a strong desire to hear about sin, judgment, and then the amazing grace and mercy given in Jesus Christ. You cannot remove anything from the gospel when people are coming to faith in Christ, because God is the one drawing them by His Holy Spirit in convicting them of their sins.

Therefore, the entire Word of God is what those true seekers want to hear. If we give them programs and other worldly things and they feel satisfied, that only means God is not drawing them to Himself. They just want to add religion to their already sinful state because they don't want to repent. They are still in their sins.

So, those who don't want to hear the full Word of God don't belong to the kingdom of God. They are still in the flesh and cannot please God. Remember, Jesus warned us that many will say to Him, “Lord, Lord,” but He will say to them, “Depart from me you workers of iniquity, I never knew you”. He also said that many will seek to enter the kingdom, but will not be able, because they are going on the broad way (religion; **Matthew 7:13**).

I believe the "seeker-sensitive" movement is part of the broad way that leads many to destruction. This is a method developed by man, but preaching the offense of the cross is the way of God. The gospel is not sensitive to sinners; it's offensive and without apology.

Now, if we preach the Word of God and they are offended, we are to shake the dust from off our feet. It is expected that many will be offended. All we must do is continue to preach the gospel and God will save His elect. Remember, not every person is going to heaven and is willing to accept and believe the gospel.

The book of Acts tells us in **Chapter 2:47** that "the Lord added to the church daily such as should be saved." It is the Lord who does the work of salvation by His Spirit and sovereign election, not us by our "seeker-sensitive" methods. Salvation is a mystery beyond us, which God performs.

We cannot speak to the human heart, only the Spirit of God can do that. Even though we would like to see everyone in Heaven, most will be in Hell. I am not saying this from my own personal view, Jesus did. He said: "Many are called, but few are chosen" (**Matthew 22:14**). In another passage, He also says that many follow the broad way that leads to destruction (**Matthew 7:13–14**).

I will believe what Jesus said and not what man thinks. So, there is only one method to bring people to God, and that's preaching. I'm not talking about just preaching the love of God; the apostles preach the cross of Christ, the full counsel on eternal judgment, faith, and mercy.

Preaching should therefore bring glory to God by proclaiming His entire Word, showing God as amazingly holy as no other, and high and lifted up far above the heavens in His perfect holiness. Knowing this, the church service should then be geared towards bringing glory to God in worshipping Him in the beauty of holiness; in spirit and in truth. It should not be geared towards avoiding offense to sinners.

How should we have a church service?

In today's church services, many have deviated from the Scriptures and invented their own methods of worship, not prescribed by God. We have forgotten what a church service is about. If we don't do what we are supposed to do, we will quench the Holy Spirit, and the power of God will not be in the church.

We must know the following:

1. The church is the body of Christ and is made up of those in the kingdom of God: born again of the Holy Spirit.
2. It is for believers who assembly to worship God in Spirit and in truth.
3. The church service is for the worship of God, and the building up of the saints through the proclamation of God's Word.
4. The church of God is where the Word of God is preached in its fullness, nothing left out. Saints are edified and exhorted, and sin is rebuked and dealt with.
5. God is exalted for His holiness and righteousness as revealed in Jesus Christ through the cross.
6. God is also exalted for His righteous judgment that He will bring on those who reject Christ, disobey the gospel, persecute His

people, and try to destroy His church.

7. The church service should be geared towards glorifying God's holy name, and praising Him for salvation.
8. God's church does not conform or change to adapt to culture or society.
9. The church service is not to please men, but God.
10. The church is insensitive to how sinners feel. It does not change to please sinners, because it's a holy place that has its own rules set out by a holy God, whose righteousness is very high above the heavens and separate from sinners, and whose ways are contrary to ours.
11. For sinners to be a part of the church, they must repent and be conformed into the likeness of Christ. If not, they don't belong there; they can leave; it's not their Father's house.

Why would anyone feel at ease at his enemy's house? If anyone is a friend of the world, he is an enemy of God. Some might get angry at this statement, but that's what the Bible says in **James 4:4.**

Jesus Christ is the head of the Church, His body, and sets the rules on how the service is to be carried out. He sets the rules on how members are to live and glorify Him. These rules are not to be changed by anyone to please men simply because they are afraid of offending sinners. God will bring judgment on leaders who try to please men by being seeker-sensitive.

The gospel is offensive and that's just the way it is. Jesus Christ came to His own, but His own did not receive Him. He offended many. It is no different today. Many people will say they love God, but they just don't love His rules. You cannot love God and then not listen to and obey what He says. You must do what God says, and not what you want. So, the preacher is not to give people what they want to hear, but what God says they must do, even if they are offended.

For example, in the Old Testament, God brought judgment on Nadab and Abihu, when they disobeyed Him on how to worship in the temple. They offered the wrong fire and died as a result. They tried to change the worship service by doing it their way, and God brought judgment. Why did God do that to these priests? Because God is holy and we are to worship Him in the beauty of holiness. We cannot worship God in our own way; it's very dangerous! Don't experiment with the worship service of God.

In the Old Testament, the order of service for the tabernacle was given to Moses and was to be followed exactly as given by God. The priests could not just go into the most holy place and do whatever they wanted to do; they could die. They had to do it exactly as God told them.

The priests could not profane the name of the Lord by standing before God without recognizing His holy name. They had to fear His name and perform the ordinances as given in the Law, and worship Him in the beauty of holiness. They had to constantly think about the holiness of God when approaching Him. It was a matter of life or death if they dared to stand in front of God on their own terms and presumed, that God would accept and even be pleased with their worship.

Now we get to the New Testament period of grace and have formulated the idea that because we are no longer under the Law, we can change the service and not be so much concerned about God bringing judgment. This is not true. **Hebrews 10** tells us that we are under more serious judgment because of the blood of the Son of God. For example, if we take the communion without discerning the Lord's body, we could die (sleep; **1 Corinthians 11:30**). Ananias and Sapphira died for lying to the Holy Ghost, and that was in the New Testament.

Remember, judgment begins at the house of God. We have forgotten that God is still holy and that His Church belongs to Him and He is the Head, not us. He will root up and throw down everything that does not line up with His holy name. He is still the same God whose holiness endures forever, and His righteousness shall never be abolished.

We see how the apostles and early Christians in the book of Acts carried out a church service, and that's what we should do. They continued steadfastly in certain doctrines, without wavering. They didn't try to be inventive in worship. It was simple and straight to the point, constantly and consistently. They were greatly persecuted, but they did not waver. They died for what they believed in.

Acts 2:42: *And they continued stedfastly in the apostles' doctrine and fellowship, and in breaking of bread, and in prayers.*

Acts 2:46–47: *And they, continuing daily with one accord in the temple, and breaking bread from house to house, did eat their meat with gladness and singleness of heart, Praising God, and having favour with all the people. And the Lord added to the church daily such as should be saved.*

The first Christians were daily in one accord in the temple, and from house to house, continuing steadfastly in the apostles' doctrine, breaking bread with one heart, and praising God, and the Lord added to the church daily such as should be saved. These are the things they did, and the Lord saved those who were to be added to His church, and healed those who were sick.

In view of the early church, are we following the pattern set out by the apostles? Or have we moved away? First, they were bonded together by the Holy Spirit of God on the same ground, the cross of Christ. Secondly, they broke bread together from house to house, which means they always remembered the body that was broken for them, the Lord's body. Thirdly, they continued steadfastly in the apostles' doctrine and prayers.

What doctrine of the apostles did the church continue in?

If you go through the New Testament, especially in the book of **Acts**, you will see that the apostles all preached Jesus Christ. The Apostle Peter's first sermon proclaimed Jesus as the one the prophets wrote about in all the Scriptures. He expounded the books of the Old

Testament to show that they're all about Jesus. In other words, they preached Jesus Christ. The Apostle Peter preached that Jesus, whom the rulers crucified, is both "Lord and Christ".

Acts 2:36: *Therefore let all the house of Israel know assuredly, that God hath made that same Jesus, whom ye have crucified, both Lord and Christ.*

Acts 5:42: *And daily in the temple, and in every house, they ceased not to teach and preach Jesus Christ.*

They proclaimed Jesus as the Messiah, Son of God, God in the flesh, the Maker of heaven and earth, the only Savior, the Judge of the living and the dead, the only way of salvation. The Apostle Paul was immensely persecuted for preaching Jesus Christ as being the One whom all the Scriptures reveal. He made his numerous defenses before kings, showing that Jesus was the fulfillment of the Law of Moses, and that the Law pointed to Christ. He proved from Scriptures that salvation was only by grace through faith in Christ alone; that Jesus is the Hope of Israel and the world.

In other words, they preached Jesus Christ as the healer, God the Savior (Jesus), the righteousness of God revealed from heaven, and the One exalted at the right hand of God with all power and dominion over all creation. They made it known that if anyone rejected Jesus Christ, eternal judgment was the result, and that it was very serious.

In summary, the gospel of Christ reveals that everything ever written by all the prophets, including the Law of Moses, the ceremonies and ordinances in the Old Testament, the Psalms, Proverbs, and all other Scriptures were fulfilled in Jesus Christ, and that all things reside in Him. He is the Word of God. In other words, to look at the Word of God is to look at Jesus.

He is the only salvation of God, the Judge of all mankind and angels, the Giver of eternal life, the King of all kings, the Creator of all things, the Lamb of God who takes away the sins of the world, the Sabbath rest, the true sacrifice for sins, the only hope of the world, the joy of the world, the peace of the world, and the One and only True God who is to be worshipped, praised, loved, adored, and exalted. He is before all things and He holds all things by His own mighty power.

Acts 28:31: *Preaching the kingdom of God, and teaching those things which concern the Lord Jesus Christ, with all confidence, no man forbidding him.*

CHAPTER 20

PREPARING AND EXPECTING THE GLORIOUS RETURN OF CHRIST

Be always ready to meet Jesus when He returns.

Are you ready to meet the Lord Jesus? When Christ returns to judge the world, will you be confident to face Him with joy, or will you face Him with terror? Those who are right with God will face Jesus with joy, while those who are not right with God will face Him with terror.

The righteous are those who have believed in Jesus and are cleansed from their sins by the blood that Jesus shed on the cross; only they can face Him with joy and confidence. There is absolutely no other way to be made right with God other than through the shed blood of Jesus Christ.

The unrighteous are those who don't believe in Jesus and have refused to come to Him to be cleansed from their sins in His shed blood. These are the ones who fail to believe that Jesus is God made visible in human form. They have refused to believe and obey Jesus and will face Him with terror on Judgment Day.

In case you believe that people will end up in hell because they have done horrible sins, that's not true: people go to hell because they don't believe in Jesus. They rejected the cross as foolishness and unnecessary in justifying sinners as righteous before a holy God, and now have nothing to cover their sins. Fig leaves (religion) cannot do it.

John 16:7–11: *Nevertheless I tell you the truth; It is expedient for you that I go away: for if I go not away, the Comforter will not come unto you; but if I depart, I will send him unto you. And when he is come, he will reprove the world of sin, and of righteousness, and of judgment: Of sin, because they believe not on me; Of righteousness, because I go to my Father, and ye see me no more; Of judgment, because the prince of this world is judged.*

John 5:39–40: *Search the scriptures; for in them ye think ye have eternal life: and they are they which testify of me. And ye will not come to me, that ye might have life.*

Listen to what Jesus said in the gospel of John. He said if He did not come, they would not have been condemned guilty of sin, but because He came and they had hated Him, now they had nothing to cover their sin. (He is the only covering for sin; that's the point.)

John 15:22–23: *If I had not come and spoken unto them, they had not had sin: but now they have no cloke for their sin. He that hateth me hateth my Father also.*

The only way to be right with God and have a perfect covering for your sins, where God is well pleased to call you righteous and holy, is through the cross of Jesus Christ. There is absolutely no other way. That's what the Lord God Almighty has said that we all must do to face Him with joy. Who are you to think that you can disobey what the Creator of the universe has said, and believe you will stand before God justified as righteous?

Because Jesus is the Lord God Almighty who is also the Judge of the universe, He has promised to return shortly to reward both the righteous and the unrighteous. So, you need to make sure you are cleansed from your sins in His blood.

Now is the day to be saved. You should note that you are living on the edge of eternity. You don't know when you will die or when Christ will suddenly appear. You don't want to face Jesus as Judge, so make sure you are prepared to meet Him in His righteousness.

1 Thessalonians 5:2–4: *For yourselves know perfectly that the day of the Lord so cometh as a thief in the night. For when they shall say, Peace and safety; then sudden destruction cometh upon them, as travail upon a woman with child; and they shall not escape. But ye, brethren, are not in darkness, that that day should overtake you as a thief.*

Revelation 16:15: *Behold, I come as a thief. Blessed is he that watcheth, and keepeth his garments, lest he walk naked, and they see his shame.*

Matthew 24:44: *Therefore be ye also ready: for in such an hour as ye think not the Son of man cometh.*

How can you be ready? What must you do to be ready?

You need to be born again of the Spirit of God. You must repent of your sins and call upon Jesus to save you.

This was what the Philippian jailor did. After God shook the prison and loosed the chains from off the prisoners, the warden became very afraid and asked the Apostle Paul and Barnabas how to be saved, as follows:

Acts 16:30–31: *And brought them out, and said, Sirs, what must I do to be saved? And they said, Believe on the Lord Jesus Christ, and thou shalt be saved, and thy house.*

Upon hearing the gospel, the prison warden repented of his sins, called upon Jesus to save him, and was baptized along with his entire family the same night. He cried out to God to save him and his family because of what he saw God do that night in shaking terribly the prison.

Romans 10:9–10: *That if thou shalt confess with thy mouth the Lord Jesus, and shalt believe in thine heart that God hath raised him from the dead, thou shalt be saved. For with the heart man believeth unto righteousness; and with the mouth confession is made unto salvation.*

If you fear God and the judgment that you deserve for your sins, why don't you come to the cross today? Salvation is freely available through the blood of Christ, the blood that God Himself paid to redeem you. You don't have to work for it. But you must repent and put your faith in Christ.

Recognize that the righteous judgment for your sins is eternal death. Be willing and mournful about your sins. In other words, repent of your sins. Call upon the Lord Jesus and He will cleanse you and forgive you of all your sins (see **1 John 1:9**). No sin is too difficult that He will not forgive. He took the place of Barabbas, a murderer, when He went to the cross, demonstrating that even a murderer can be saved (**Mark 15:7–15**). Also, he saved the thief who called out to Him on the cross (**Luke 23:43**). How amazing is His love and forgiveness! Anyone can be saved!

Lightning Source UK Ltd.
Milton Keynes UK
UKHW02f0619301117
313578UK00006B/152/P

9 781603 835510